MILES MURPHY

MILES MURPHY

WHO RESCUED WHOM?

PHILIP CASALE

MILES MURPHY
WHO RESCUED WHOM?

iUniverse books may be ordered through booksellers or by contacting:

iUniverse
1663 Liberty Drive
Bloomington, IN 47403
www.iuniverse.com
1-800-Authors (1-800-288-4677)

Because of the dynamic nature of the Internet, any web addresses or links contained in this book may have changed since publication and may no longer be valid. The views expressed in this work are solely those of the author and do not necessarily reflect the views of the publisher, and the publisher hereby disclaims any responsibility for them.

Any people depicted in stock imagery provided by Thinkstock are models, and such images are being used for illustrative purposes only. Certain stock imagery © Thinkstock.

ISBN: 978-1-5320-3185-4 (sc)
ISBN: 978-1-5320-3186-1 (e)

Library of Congress Control Number: 2017916569

Print information available on the last page.

iUniverse rev. date: 10/28/2017

To those individuals who have rescued a shelter dog
    And to those who have been rescued by that dog

For the nearly 3.3 million dogs that are projected to enter United States' shelters in 2017,
    A home is just a reader's choice away

A Note From the Author

There's something special about having a dog. And for the first twenty-seven years of my life, I never knew what it felt like to have man's best friend by my side, though I had always imagined what it would be like.

After graduating from veterinary school in Oklahoma, I returned to the East Coast to practice veterinary medicine and to begin the search for my first dog. It wasn't before long that my dream would become a reality.

As a small-animal veterinarian, I have seen thousands of dogs with different personalities, appearances, stories and histories, but objectively speaking, there has not been one like our rescue dog, Miles Murphy.

In the coming chapters I will introduce you to my family, my wife, and our first of many eye-opening encounters with Miles. Fortunately, the mischievous behavior and daily head-scratching moments were always accompanied by the everyday joys of having this special dog. But it was the unprecedented happiness and countless memories that had a lasting impact on our lives and instilled the values of this unique animal-human bond.

And that's why I decided to share his story.

Welcome to Oklahoma

"It was the best of times, it was the worst of times, it was the age of wisdom, it was the age of foolishness, it was the epoch of belief, it was the epoch of incredulity, it was the season of light, it was the season of darkness, it was the spring of hope, it was the winter of despair."
— Charles Dickens, *A Tale of Two Cities*

Being in veterinary school was not always easy. Being in veterinary school in Oklahoma made it that much harder. The transition from the North East to the Midwest sounded alright on paper. A change of scenery, warmer weather and the occasional tornado – I guess it could be worse. I was just going to be studying and taking tests for the next four years anyway, right? How hard could that be to do it 1,430 miles from home? Hell, going to Oklahoma State University versus one of the Ivy League schools was going to save me over $100,000. That put a temporary smile on my face then. Actually, it still does today.

August 14, 2009. Well, when I dropped my best friend Sarah off at Tulsa International Airport and began my 94 mile drive back to the campus in Stillwater, there was plenty of time to ponder about life. Reluctantly, there was time to think about my progressively unhealthy, 57-year-old mother being taken care of by my rapidly aging and tiring 58-year-old father. Over the next four years of schooling, the home front would be filled with difficulty, but tough mindedness on my parents' behalf. My mother would seemingly be in and out of her doctors' office more often than my dad would be in his work office. A hip replacement, dislocated hip, fractured femur, broken ankle and a battered mind, all of which wreaked the damages inflicted by her post-menopausal, osteoporotic skeleton, had put an even greater demand on my dad's Catholic based, inner strength. Prior to our three day, cross-country drive to Oklahoma, Sarah and I could envision what the future challenges looked like, but we did not even mention it or bother putting any energy toward discussing the disheartening inevitable.

Ok, back to that first drive from Tulsa's airport.

There was time to think about the upcoming months of separation between me and Sarah. Leading up to that day, I never once doubted my devotion to her or whether our relationship would work. I'm not just saying that either. Simply put, that was not part of my mindset, and I had no intentions of allowing it to creep in then. That included the night I took the first of many lonesome drives back from the airport. Having said that, I tried to distract myself and think about anything else on my nearly two-hour drive that was uplifting such as Yankees baseball. Then it dawned on me as I flipped through the static filled radio, I no longer got 880 AM NY, the Yankees radio network. The reason I did not have reception was because I was hundreds of miles away. Duh. It's easy to let that slip your mind when for the past eight summer years driving, play-by-plan announcer John Sterling and color-commentator Suzyn Waldman were there calling your favorite team's game at the press of a button. More importantly, the reason there was static on every station was because dark, ominous clouds had surrounded my 2002 Hyundai Accent. I was now driving 85 mph down Route 35, a major highway en-route to Stillwater that was surrounded by empty dried-grass fields with an occasional oil pump and herd of beef cattle. The harder I pressed the accelerator, the faster the storm clouds enclosed my car. What was the likelihood that on my first solo night in the state of Oklahoma that I would be so lucky? There was not going to be any outrunning of this storm, for within minutes the weather gave a whole new meaning to five o'clock shadow. Golf-ball sized hail, minimal visibility, and 60 mph gusts of wind made my car feel like a tumbleweed in the middle of a prairie. The only thing I could see through my pelted windshield was the occasional dotted line on the highway and the precipitation bouncing off the hood of my 'Black Beauty,' my appropriately nicknamed car. I recalled how in New Jersey there was an exit at least every one to two miles on major highways. Well, in the Midwest I quickly learned that there could be no rest-stops for tens of miles and that you can drive a long way before seeing civilization let alone a building to cower inside during a storm. Welcome to Oklahoma.

By the way, there was no power on my first night in the town of Stillwater. *How many days until Christmas break,* I pondered.

131. Not that I was counting.

CHAPTER 1

And So It Begins...

"Acquiring a dog may be the only time a person gets to choose a relative."
— Mordecai Siegal, author

July 28, 2013. An afternoon drizzle fell onto the town of Mount Olive, New Jersey. The roads were damp as I made a right turn into the gravel-parking lot of the 11th Hour Animal Shelter on that mid-August afternoon. This wooden, two building complex was the home to a few dozen abandoned dogs and cats – and I was here to rescue one. As I parked the car in the makeshift parking lot buried in the woods, I sat there in the driver's seat and reminisced.

As my mind began to drift, I recalled the previous twenty-seven years, a four-decade span of time when every birthday list or Christmas letter to either Santa or eventually mom and dad routinely included one request: a dog. As a child in elementary school, my parents told me that I was too young, too irresponsible to take care of an animal. They felt that *they* would be the ones to take care of *my* pet. Late night walks, veterinary visits, the demands of 'pet-hood.' The list went on and on as to why this was not the time. I always thought that my dad detested animals. For him, the thought of having a furry, four-legged slobbering, shedding, shaking, barking creature scuffing up the oak floors on the inside of his quiet, tidy home or urine-scalding the grass on his front yard would be unimaginable. Having said that, as a young kid, I always felt that I could work my 'mommy' over, to have her convince my 'father' that I would be responsible and trustworthy. I would butter her up, help with chores, make my bed, clean off my dinner plate, and put my toys away with the ultimate goal of showcasing my maturity at the grand old age of eight. But to no avail.

The same trend continued into middle school, but the odds did not grow in my favor, as both of my parents were then working. My dad, Frank, was commuting into New York City, waking up at 5:00 am to get the 6:23 am Man's Transit train from Whitehouse Station, NJ to Penn Station. The field of information technology was continuing to blossom, and his career at a leading worldwide enterprise and subsequent paycheck were flourishing as a result. My mom was a substitute teacher at the local elementary school. With both of them out of the house by 7:30 AM, I realized that my chances had all but diminished. Then as I entered high school, made the Honor Roll, became the President of the French Honor Society, and built my academic resume for acceptance into college, the trend continued. Was I more responsible, mature, and trustworthy? Yes. But in their eyes, with me leaving the homeland for college, my dad did not want to get stuck pet-sitting when all the other birds had left the nest. Do you think anything changed when I was in college? Of course not. My dad would always say "I'll let you have a dog when I know of a good vet." Ten years later, I was on the verge of taking him up on that offer...

A sudden knock on the passenger window broke my train of thought. "Are you coming? It's starting to pour," Sarah asked.

The rain was filtering through the overlying trees onto the roof of my car. As I got out of the car, we bolted over to the first building where we had mutually arranged to meet Tina, a volunteer for the organization, at 10:00 AM. The door was locked so we scrambled over to the adjacent building where to our disappointment we found that door to be closed as well. Of course, I knew where this was going.

"Are you sure that this is the right time?" Sarah questioned with a frustrating glance.

I really wanted to say, "No, I'm not sure. I drove you forty-five minutes out here on your weekend off at the wrong time just to aggravate you." In the meantime the puddles were forming on the gravel by the entrance way to each building, in part due to the fact there were no gutters on the roof so the water just continued to waterfall around the perimeter of the building.

After a couple of minutes of evading puddles and looking for another entrance, the door at the top of the steps in the second building swung open.

"Good morning, you must be Phil and Sarah." A woman in her mid-forties wearing an 11th Hour Shelter sweatshirt and a nametag that read 'Tina' approached us with her right hand extended. She apologized for the moat surrounding the building and led us up to the main office. After taking a seat on the couch, we received some pointers on the importance of animal care, the value of a pet, and oh yeah, we were briefly interrogated on our plans for our new addition.

"Where is Miles going to be staying?" Tina asked, pen in hand, eager to etch our response into the formal documents of 11th Hour Shelter.

"206 Captain's Woods Road, in Whitehouse Station," I quickly responded. That was a bit of a fabrication, in part because that was the address for my parents. There was no chance that I would put my apartment address on the paper, because then she would be calling the apartment, verifying weight restrictions, pet acceptances, yada yada. Figuring the new luxury apartment complex where we were now living had only recently adopted a pet-friendly policy on dogs thirty-five pounds and under, I was all but certain that our new furry friend would surpass that limit. Getting evicted in the first week of having my first dog would be a problem. Simply put, I was not going to give the leasing office a heads-up by telling Tina that I was going to be bringing our unregistered-dog to 445 Horizon Circle in the coming hours.

I wanted to get this over with. Tina was not helping me in that regard as the plethora of questions continued. We wrapped up the twenty-minute question and answer session with some one-sided lecturing on the importance of veterinary visits and heartworm prevention.

"Have you decided on a veterinarian in your area?" Tina continued.

Yeah, me, I thought to myself. I wanted to tell her that she could stop the monologue. I do this for a living. With that in mind, this was the perfect example of when less is more. Do not say anything, keep it short and sweet. By the way, it is illegal for a veterinarian to treat his own dog, not that I was planning on it.

"No, not yet," Sarah replied. "We have discussed some possibilities."

After jotting down a few checkmarks and notes in our file, Tina placed the folder on the coffee table, and wheeled her office chair over to the computer to begin entering our information from the questionnaire sheet that we had previously filled out prior to coming. She called into the next room and asked Samantha the anticipated question, "Would you like to go get Miles?" Out from an enclosed room emerged Sam, a volunteer wearing a Mount Olive High School sweatshirt. I'd say she had to be no older than seventeen, mostly because of her school apparel, young complexion, five-foot stature and one-hundred-pound frame. Walking across the room, she acknowledged us with a simple smile and grabbed an umbrella in the basket next to the front door. Stepping outside, Sam put the umbrella to use, visually mapped out her pathway, making the vigilant decision to dodge the puddles as she hurried across the parking lot in the direction of the first building.

I could not believe that within a handful of minutes my twenty-seven-year long dream of having a dog would finally come true. I squirmed in my wooden chair waiting patiently, full of anticipation. I don't get giddy, but I was as excited as I would ever let on to be. My demeanor was calm, but I remember that the stoic shell of my exterior was struggling to muffle the increasing intensity of my heart beat. Sarah and I were small talking, essentially conversing about nothing in an attempt to alleviate the nervousness that was due to uncertain expectations. Sarah was making me anxious, in part because of her unknowing overuse of nervous laughter. Seriously, is the question, 'Where are we going to put his crate' that funny? Maybe in this circumstance, yes.

"Here he comes!" Sarah expressed with her unperfected, yet characteristic nervous elation.

From the overlooking window, we could see the front door to the first building swing open. Like a stallion out of the gates at the Kentucky Derby, we saw Miles bolt out of the kennel, dragging Sam by the leash. She did not have her umbrella. So much for avoiding puddles and keeping those shoes dry. He looked like a sled dog from the Iditarod as he mushed across the lot and up the steps. The vision of him running up the steps faded behind the cover of the wall and was replaced by the sound of panting being altered by the pull of the collar around his neck.

As the door opened, there he stood. Literally. With his open mouth and droopy tongue, Miles was hopping on his rear legs, flailing his outstretched front paws, and making Sam struggle to hold back his inner rearing bronco.

"You're free," Sarah explained as Sam unclipped the leash from his collar. And was he ever. Talk about happiness, he was jumping and running around this 15' x 15' room as if he had just been released from captivity. Oh, well I guess the cement-floored, 3' x 3' x 3' steel-framed kennel that he had just spent the past 4 months in would do that to anyone or anything. It was fun to see him release his 2-year-old energy. He raced over to Sarah and nuzzled his nose under Sarah's extended hands. His white-tipped tail whipped back and forth as I rubbed his sides. His ribs were noticeable in the right lighting, but I did not recall them to be as easily visible in the past as they were that day. Not surprising though. For one, he was soaking wet, and two, he had been living in a shelter.

Slipping on the floor as he ran around the room, he could not contain himself. The bright white fur on all four paws contrasted so perfectly against the deep black of his coat as I sat and admired his prancing gait. He raced around Tina's desk and darted across the room. Smells in that corner, sniffs in this area. He had an enthusiasm for life that had been succumbed by the anxiety of abandonment. And now it was coming out.

And it was still coming out ten minutes later as Tina approached us to sign some paperwork that just came out of the printer.

"Out of there," exclaimed Tina, as she pulled back on Miles who was head first in her office garbage can. "I had just eaten breakfast so he probably smells something."

She handed us the contract to read over. Essentially it read, once you take him, he's yours. No refunds. That's right, shelters have bills too. Who do you think pays for the Purina One dog food, building costs, and veterinary care? Donations only go so far. That is if they are fortunate to receive any.

Once again Tina had to remove Miles face from the garbage. The lure of the crust from almond battered French toast and scrambled eggs had drawn him near. This time, however, she placed the lid over the top of the container to control the temptation.

I noticed that Miles' weight on the contract read forty-four pounds. Damn. If I was ever in a circumstance where I needed to register him at the apartment complex, he would be turned down. Noticing a scale in the back left corner of the room, I asked if we could reweigh him.

Forty-five pounds. My eyes quickly shifted to Sarah in disappointment. At that point, there wasn't much we could do about it. I could just feel Tina wondering why I was so intrigued by his weight. I knew she was not going to change the number on the contract to read thirty-five pounds. Why would she? In her eyes, why would I want that? Keeping in mind my motto, 'less is more,' I quickly pivoted.

"Do I make the check payable to 11th Hour Shelter?" I questioned as I motioned for Sarah's purse.

"No need to pay, Chris already took care of it for you. You just need to sign," Tina replied.

Chris Dremousky was a neighbor who lived a few houses down from my parents from the time that I was ten years old. At the time she was in her mid-thirties and worked for a major insurance company and lived with her long-time boyfriend, John Scarva, an executive manager of a construction insurance provider. Since both worked demanding jobs, she had been on the lookout for a dog-walker to take care of her two dogs, Harley and Sonny. At that time, Harley was a 5-year-old Shih Tzu with severe skin allergies to grass. And it didn't take long for her to live up to her reputation as being the laziest, most stubborn dog in the neighborhood. In fact, Harley would need to be carried outside just to get the engines started. I guess if my belly turned red like a tomato I wouldn't want to go for a walk around the grass cul-de-sac either. And then there was Sonny, a 12-year-old energetic Husky, who loved going outside. Imagine taking these polar opposites on a walk. Sonny, if he wasn't having seizures, enjoyed the revitalizing stroll, especially when he remembered how to put one leg in front of the other in the later years. To make a long story short, I loved the opportunity to see those dogs. I could not get home from school fast enough to race down the street to see them. Honestly, I'd prefer the serenity of that afternoon walk over the ridiculousness of after-school clubs any day of the week. The nonsense imposed by the student cronies in academia, especially in the middle school years more so than in the high school years, was difficult to become immersed in. For example, listening to the President of the Student Council leading the class in discussions on the funds for decorations for the Winter Snowflake Ball at a Tuesday afternoon meeting was difficult to hear. Now you can understand, right? Sonny and Harley were like my pets, for at least thirty minutes every afternoon, Monday through Friday. When I first started my dog walking business in 1996, my dad had said that the novelty would wear off. Well, after a total of five dogs over the course of twelve years at this one house alone, it never did.

And, did I mention I was paid. And paid well. Thirty dollars a week was a lot of money for me back in the mid '90s. Plus, when Chris was home on an occasional Friday afternoon, or payday, thirty bucks would turn into two twenties if she didn't have the precise amount of cash on hand. Only if Jay knew that Chris was handing out change like candy on Halloween. Over the years including the summer and winter breaks during college, I would continue to take their 'children' out for a walk. And as the years went by, my rates went up. Hey, it's business.

In the recent months, Chris had told me about 11th Hour Shelter, in part because she had been volunteering with them for the past year. I just so happened to scroll through their website one night and saw Miles' picture. Of course I mentioned him to Sarah and Chris. After all was said and done, and without us knowing, Chris surprised me with a graduation gift that was twenty-seven years in the making.

I looked at Sarah, who did not know this was coming. In fact, Sarah's intention as of August 2009, my first year of veterinary school, was to buy me my first dog upon graduation. We were both surprised to say the least.

After signing my name on the dotted line, it was official. Miles was now part of our family.

In the meantime, Miles continued to scavenge around the floor, sniffing at every nook and cranny he could discover. His intrigue and investigation led him to a folded pile of fresh linens. It wasn't before long that his mouth displayed the newly discovered folded towel out of its corners. Fortunately, Sam had been watching him from the laundry room and took it out of the vice grip of his jaws. Unfortunately, she placed it on the chair where Miles quickly retrieved it and began to think it was a game of hide and seek. This game needed to come to an end.

"Miles, do you want to go outside? Do you want to go home?" Sarah joyfully asked as Sam handed her a shiny chain-linked leash from the wall.

"He needs a metal one because he chews through the vinyl ones," Sam smiled politely.

Dropping the towel, Miles pranced towards the rattling of the leash and in between the side-to-side miniature hops, Sarah attached his leash and headed to the great outdoors. As evident from earlier in the morning, Miles' enthusiasm had no regard for the weather. He frolicked across the parking lot, leading Sarah into the muddy woods, where in part, the trees provided some cover from the rain falling clouds. Miles had done his best to ensure that his paws touched every area of mud as possible as he found his route to my car.

As I opened the back right passenger door, Miles eagerly jumped in as Sarah let go of his leash. I wondered what he was thinking. When was the last time he was in a car? Where does he think he's going? I did recall one of my earlier phone conversations with Tina when she told me that Miles had car sickness the first three times he was transported in the shelter van. *I guess we're going to find out real quick if that's still the case*, I thought.

I closed the car door carefully, ensuring that Miles' tail and all extremities were well protected. The last thing I needed was to spend the rest of Sunday at the emergency veterinary hospital after having my dog for ten minutes. After I went around to the driver's side, I peered through the window and saw his big brown eyes staring at me from his curled up position. He looked like he was half the size.

"Aww, you're so cute," Sarah remarked as she turned around in her seat.

For a dog that was always active, jumping, and borderline-rambunctious, I thought this was way too easy. Was this the same dog that was running around the office with a towel in his mouth? At the four separate occasions that I interacted with Miles, I did not see him sit or lay down once. Could he be tired? Who was he kidding? Two-year-old border collies don't get tired. I'm sure he was just innocently sitting there while he mentally fine-tuned his next deceptive act.

The skies remained overcast and the drizzle continued to fall as we transitioned from the gravel-covered parking lot to the highway pavement of Route 46. Our destination was my parent's home, now known as grandma and grandpa's when in the presence of Miles. Tongue in cheek, I'm sure my dad was going to like me referring to him as an elder statesman and fast-forwarding him into the golden years. The last thing my dad needed was to be reminded of father time, that is as he continued to work a full-time job both in his IT office and at home taking care of the house chores and my mom. But if I could put a smile on his face, it would be worth the occasional sly comment, or two.

Less than a minute into the nearly thirty-five minute drive, my inner thoughts came to an end as I could feel the warmth of a light pant next to my right ear. As my eyes quickly jolted up to the rear-view mirror, I could see the newest co-pilot of the Black Beauty. Looking sideways, there he stood. His front paws' nails were embedded on the center console, his eyes peered stoically ahead, and his broad chest thrust forward as he captained his four-wheeled ship down the highway.

CHAPTER 2

Going to...Grandma and Grandpa's?

"Home is the place where, when you have to go there, they have to take you in."
— Robert Frost, author

The grass is always greener on the other side of the fence.

This classic idiom may apply to anyone or anything, that is, except when we're talking about my father's lawn.

My dad has always emphasized the importance of keeping up the appearance of the outside of the house. He says, and rightfully so, that it adds value to the home, increases curb appeal, and earns some street cred amongst the critics, also known as *the neighbors*. To him, it all starts with the grass, particularly the front lawn.

Growing up I recall the pure giddiness that my dad would try to contain when he would wake up on a spring Sunday morning, oh around 6 AM, to begin fertilizing the lawn. Yes, to fertilize the lawn.

"We need a healthy lawn this fall,' my father would state to my mom, which only caused her to grow more disgusted that he was waking up early on the weekend to take care of the lawn rather than treat us out to breakfast. Applying that fertilizer would put a smile on his face like Christmas morning for a child. The only way to one-up that bi-annual feeling was to mow the lawn on a weekly basis.

I learned over the years that there is a science to mowing the lawn. It's called 'follow your father's instructions.' The mowing pattern, the time of the day, and the height of the blades of grass all contribute to the art of lawn care. Zzz, you still with me? Well, as a kid growing up, I cannot tell you the number of times this was discussed. We're not even going to talk about edging, sprinkler systems, or mulching of the shrub beds, but trust me when I say it follows the same pattern.

When I was about six years old I remember how my dad laid sod on the front lawn. And I also remember when he came home from work the next day to find my older brother Frank playing five on five tackle football with friends from middle school. As a result, the newly laid sod had visibly shifted and exposed gaping areas of soil. Sections of grass were raised and some of the sod had moved off onto the sidewalk and driveway. My dad was so pissed. I saw him boiling over inside. And the neighbors verbally heard those visualizations.

Over the years, the only thing that would sour a backyard barbeque or baseball catch with him would be the discovery of a section of crab grass or brown patch of grass. But that was only temporary as the disappointment was eventually replaced by the elation that there was another outdoor project involving soil, seed, and his hands. He could easily and gleefully spend a whole weekend taking care of the outdoors. One could see how much my dad loved his lawn and still does to this day.

Enter Miles, my new co-captain.

The thought of having Miles on my dad's, uh um, my parents' lawn was mind-blowing. Imagining him relieving himself in the center portion of the front yard and my dad's ensuing ire brought a smirk to my face. That expression was quickly replaced by a blank stare as the vision of seeing Miles *inside* of the home entered my mind. I envisioned him running around the house like a bull in a china shop. Scratched floors, ripped couches, stolen food from the table would not go over well in the Casale household. And my dad would personally be escorting Miles back out to the car.

We pulled into the recently resealed driveway of my parents' two story, brick front colonial. Located on one quarter of an acre, the small property gave my dad no excuses for maintaining his outdoor standards. The house on the outside looked meticulous. I wasn't expecting anything but a well-groomed landscape, though I admittedly wouldn't guarantee that it would stay like that. All bets were off. Turning around in my seat, I locked eyes with Miles, wishing that he could interpret my look. I could only hope that this would go well. After taking him down the street to do his business, being careful to avoid any green grass associated with 206 Captain's Woods Road, we stepped foot onto my parents' porch and rang the doorbell.

"Miles sit. Miles sit. *MILES SIT!*" I shouted sternly as Sarah held onto his chain, the white tip of his tail moving back and forth like a rattlesnake.

My dad, wearing his characteristic summer apparel including denim shorts and a New York Yankees t-shirt, swung open the door, which unleashed the beast's inner excitement and tested Sarah's upper body strength. Just like earlier in the day at the shelter, Miles' internal stallion reared itself once again as he began hopping on his back legs while pawing with his outstretched front paws.

"Well hello Miles," my dad chuckled as the newest family member bounced around the front porch, unable to contain his exuberant behavior. His nails latched on to the skin on my dad's left forearm, which he used as a cane to help him stay upright. As my dad squatted down to introduce himself to his grandson, Miles lunged and nudged his muzzle into my dad's face.

"Whoa," my dad exclaimed as his large frame glasses shifted on his face. Using her body weight, Sarah pulled back, but two seconds too late. Cutaneous scratches and slobbered glasses were a result of Miles overwhelming desire to be embraced. We were off to a good start.

Miles' curiosity led him into the oak wood foyer of the house. You could hear his panting from the mailbox. There were so many rooms, smells, nooks and crannies to explore, smell, and investigate. And that meant I was going to be his shadow for the next hour. Once freed from the limitations of his leash, all bets were off.

"Hello Miles," the childish voice could be heard from down the hallway in the kitchen.

Oh no. I remember thinking that I wish I still had his leash on, but this time, *I* was two seconds too early by having already removed his restraints. Miles' head turned at the sound of my mom's voice. Her tone was like the crack of a gun to signify the start of a race. And he took off in her direction.

Holy crap, I did not want to be taking my mom to the hospital.

My mom was now using a cane as the anchor of her sixty-one-year-old, arthritic body. Having been out of the hospital only a handful of months after falling and dislocating her right hip, I did not want this to be the day that she returned. That went for my dad too, who had been doing the real heavy lifting by taking care of her for the past couple of years after multiple orthopedic surgeries. Her deteriorating physical condition continued to head in the downward direction and had started to take a toll on her mental well-being. That was accompanied by her increasing demands and expectations of my dad to do more in and out of the house. But at this moment, my thoughts were on our four-legged son racing in my mom's direction.

Gripping the kitchen chair with the hopes of softening the blow, my wide-eyed mother was left untouched, as if an unknown force pulled back on this dog's reigns. It was as if he knew that plowing through this woman would not be a wise choice for either her, or him. Phew, crisis avoided.

A couple pats on his head, and the introduction with grandma was complete. Moving along, he wandered around the newly renovated kitchen. His paws slipped around the corners as he circled the kitchen table in search of any crumbs that may have fallen on the ground.

"What else is new with you guys? How are the new jobs?" my dad asked, placing his arm around my shoulder as we headed into the kitchen. I greeted my mom with a kiss on the cheek and then headed over to the refrigerator to look for some leftovers for lunch.

We talked about my commute to the veterinary hospital from the apartment, Sarah's new nursing position, and of course, the Yankees. These were staples of my expectations for topics that would arise.

"How's my favorite nurse doing? How's the hospital?" Dad started.

"Nursing is going well. The morning drive on the highway can be a bottleneck, but what are you going to do," Sarah noted. "The floor is slightly different than what I was used to in Connecticut. Learning a new computer system, protocols, management, all of that takes time to adjust to."

"What has it been? Five years that you were working in the city?" Dad wondered.

"It's been five years?! Time goes by so fast," my mom chirped in as she placed her palm on her cheek forcing her head to the side. Her eyes darted down to the side of the center island where she could see only the back half of Miles and his wagging tail.

"And how are you Miles?" Leaning over the edge of the counter, she could see Miles face first in the white trash bin. "He's in the garbage!"

"MILES!" I reacted sternly. I was ready to yank him back by his collar when he turned around to look at me. There he was, walking towards the sound of my deafening tone and chewing on something yellow.

"Oh my..." I opened his mouth and pulled out a corn on the cob, halfway down his throat. "Are you kidding me? *ARE YOU KIDDING ME?*" I reiterated.

"Oh geez Frank, you shouldn't have left the garbage out," my mom was quick to point out blame.

"Sorry, but how am I supposed to know that he was going to get into last night's garbage," Dad responded abruptly.

My thoughts of frustration were erupting. *Come on people. This is common sense. A dog and food go hand in hand. Of course he does not know that the garbage is off limits and why, WHY, would he?*

And why are we leaving the garbage can out?

My first five minutes in the house was nearly five minutes too many. A thirty cent, half-eaten ear of corn nearly cost me $3,000 for an exploratory surgery. I couldn't believe that I turned my back for not even two minutes, and a catastrophic mess nearly developed. Throw in the fact that there were four people in one room, and this dog still found a way to bypass the human eyes into his first bout of trouble. Congratulations Miles, I'm going to watch you like a hawk.

For the next thirty minutes, we stood in the kitchen and talked about a range of topics, but I just wanted to go back to our apartment and settle in. I was anxious. My mind was everywhere but in the conversation. For the past twenty-seven years my responsibilities included schoolwork, tests, paying apartment bills, but never involved taking care of anything that was alive other than me. The palms of my hands were wet; I was assuming this was normal. Must be like the feeling new parents have when they bring home their first newborn from the hospital. Though I've never had that experience either, I'm sure it's a pretty accurate comparison. I tried to calm my nerves by reminding myself that this was what I always wanted. I figured in a few days...

"What do you think about that," Dad asked, breaking my internal thought process.

"I think it's alright, I can't complain," Sarah shrugged. I wasn't paying attention to their conversation. I guess that was my cue to get going, so I suggested to Sarah that we start thinking about going home.

We said our goodbyes, lassoed up our new addition, and headed back outdoors. While I unlocked the car door, Miles paid a visit to the green grass. It was bound to happen.

"Not my lawn. Go use the neighbor's," my dad piped in lightheartedly from his perch on the porch.

As my parents stood on the front steps and waved goodbye, I couldn't help but chuckle as I thought how that ammonia soaked soil would leave a nice patch of grass for my dad to work on next weekend.

CHAPTER 3

First Night at Home

"Home's where you go when you run out of homes."
— John le Carré, *The Honourable Schoolboy*

Dog food? Check. We had already gone the night before to the local PetSmart store and purchased a thirty-pound bag of Purina One so I could only hope that chicken and rice would be a good choice. Crate? Check. I had bought this heavy-duty crate a few weeks earlier on Amazon. Veterinarian? Not yet, but I thought I could take care of that.

Driving down route 202 was the first of many trips with a dog in my backseat. This 28th day of July marked the beginning of a minimum ten year commitment, and though we were excited, I can adamantly say that we were both nervous. It was like we had a new responsibility in our life. We now had a dependent that would need to be fed twice a day, walked three times a day, and played with countless times for at least the next decade. But this was what we agreed upon in recent weeks and now had come to fruition on this summer afternoon in 2013.

When we pulled into our apartment complex, I reminded Sarah that our new dog would need to be hidden from the management. Plain and simple. That would mean late night potty breaks under the cover of the dark of night and walks at the park rather than the apartment complex. I did not want to get evicted or have any legal or personal problems with the builders or neighbors. For whatever reason, if someone wanted to complain about our oversized dog, it would be a nightmare, especially since we wouldn't be paying the monthly pet fees.

Therefore, from the moment we turned into the development, I told Sarah that Miles needed to be out of sight and whisked into and out of the apartment as quickly as possible when no one was looking. That meant checking the hallways and the sidewalks to make sure there wasn't another resident strolling through before bringing him outside. Little did we know that our new routine, which began on that Sunday, would become routine on a daily basis over the next three years.

Fortunately, it was late in the afternoon on Sunday and management was not around as we drove past the leasing office.

"Stay down, Miles," I sternly said as I reached backwards and tried to pull down on his collar to no avail. The apartment across the parking lot from ours was under construction, but fortunately the commotion was non-existent at this time as the builders and crew were on their off day.

Miles' curiosity was refrained at first by the apprehension of stepping foot into a new environment. At first he began to sniff the corners of the wood floor entranceway. This expanded to the tiled kitchen, then the carpeted living room. New smells, sensations, sights, and sounds were different than what he was exposed to in the sterile cement kennel for the past few months. But as the night moved along, his exploration and growing familiarity with his surroundings quelled any nervousness that he may have had earlier in the day as he continued to tour the apartment.

"Bedtime Miles," I instructed as the clock struck eleven. Sarah and I were planning to sleep on the pullout sleeper sofa that night in the living room with the hope that this familiar room, which we spent the whole evening in, would provide Miles some ease for the rest of the night.

It didn't.

We were told that Miles was crate-trained, so when we set up his new home at the foot of the sofa bed, he went in with no problem.

"That was easy," I said to Sarah as he curled up in a ball in the corner of the cage. His tail tucked around and covered his muzzle as his brown eyes stared over its horizon.

"Good night Miles," Sarah whispered in her borderline baby voice. That was the last thing I heard that night before my heavy eyes closed, and I drifted off. But a little after one o'clock in the morning, my eyes opened.

Miles was whining.

"No Miles. No," I implored him, hoping that he would not wake Sarah. Well if there was any hope of us peacefully going back to bed, it was long gone when his whine transitioned to a bark.

Sarah was now up.

"I can't have this," I told her as I rolled out of bed and went over to scold Miles through the steel frame of his crate.

"What's wrong Miles? It's okay, it's okay..." Sarah consoled him.

"No, it's not okay," I cut her off. "We can't have our dog barking at one in the morning Sarah. I can't deal with that. No way. That's the one thing we talked about that he can't do. Oh yeah, by the way he's supposed to be crate-trained. If he keeps this up, he's going back."

I don't think Sarah thought I was joking at all. Because I wasn't.

As we lay back down on the sofa bed, Miles began to whine. A solitary yap followed by a series of woofs got Sarah out of bed faster than me to try and keep the peace.

"That's it, one more time I'll bring him back tomorrow," I said as my frustration began to swell.

Sarah opened up his cage door, and without a sound, Miles walked out, jumped onto the edge of the bed, and plopped down.

Is that all he wanted, I asked myself. With my head resting on my pillow, I watched him closely in full anticipation of another outburst. It never came. Seconds turned to minutes, and it wasn't before long that I gave in to the power of sleep.

It was just after six in the morning when my eyes opened. Miles was in the same spot. I fumbled for my glasses that I had rested on the arm of the sofa. When I looked back at him, I could see the white tip of his tail thrashing back and forth. I tried to ignore him but learned at that moment that once we made eye contact, all bets were off. He lunged onto my chest and rubbed his nose into my face.

The beast was awoken.

I quickly realized that the first night with Miles would be a microcosm of the years to come.

CHAPTER 4

Not What I Was Expecting

"Always expect the unexpected."
—James Patterson, American author

Sometimes it's easier to understand the present and even the future by revisiting the past. So for the next couple of chapters, I want to reflect on the months leading up to the time that Miles entered our lives to try and do just that.

May 7, 2013. Graduation day. This was the day that I had circled on my calendar nearly four years ago when I first stepped foot on the Oklahoma State University campus. To be honest, I don't know if I was more excited about earning my doctorate en route to becoming a veterinarian or knowing that the pressures and life restrictions of being a professional student for the past decade had come to an end. The days of hanging out with academic elites was over. Amen.

Veterinary school was full of students who, for the most part, were the polar opposite of me. Forget values, political and religious beliefs, or culture differences. Forget East Coast versus Midwest. Those differences were expected. Come on, I'm a center-left independent, with an Italian heritage and a New Jersey accent in the middle of the red neck, conservative Republican Bible belt. Anyone who's surprised by differences shouldn't be. In fact, I embraced this unique experience. My inner despair resonated from the letdown that even in the Midwest, academic elitism flourished just like it does in California or Philadelphia. The class was filled with many academically aristocratic, aloof individuals ballooning with an elated opinion of themselves. I recall my first physiology lecture on day one of vet school when a snobbish student from Texas turned to her newly formed clique and referred to vet school as a 'formality.' Why? Just because you were a veterinary assistant for the past couple of summers, and you think you know everything? I remember thinking to myself, *it's only going to get worse.*

This mentality, in addition to this disconnect, continued throughout the four years. Who wants to talk about horses at the bar on a Saturday night? Can't you let it go and talk about something else? Anything else? Well for some, that was clearly impossible as they burrowed themselves into their academic corners, memorizing definitions and mechanisms of actions while I understood them. I remember when a professor mentioned the 2012 Benghazi terrorist attack in Libya, and someone raised their hand to ask what that was. This news story was everywhere, for months. Figuratively speaking, could you please come out of the cave that you were living in? Perhaps read the news in between your memorization sessions. The disengagement expanded further. It was amazing how many classmates did not watch the Super Bowl or know who Derek Jeter was. Throw in the fact the blatant kiss-ass, back scratching, ego flattering behavior that many students would employ towards the professors and clinicians. I guess some people need that to try and get ahead.

But forget the previous four years. I relished the moment as my name was called to accept my diploma. Because as a modest student who always remained humble, I took pleasure not in the fact that I was graduating with honors and ranked near the top of my class, but that I was well rounded and on the verge of living life. A smile crossed my face as I reminded myself that I was that much closer to receiving my graduation gift from Sarah that was nearly three decades in the making.

It was no longer than a week from the time I completed my twenty-two hour drive home from Oklahoma that I began to go online to look for an apartment, a job, and yes, man's best friend. The first two were easy, as I was offered a near-six figure salary, full-time position working for a veterinary hospital about one half hour from my parents' home. Now the last thing I wanted to do was be in my late 20s and live at home with my mommy and daddy. Listen, my parents had always said they would keep the door open at their home for me until I found a job and my own place. I graciously took them up on their offer, but I wanted that to be a short stay. The reality was simple. I wanted to live with my best friend. The search for the apartment was easy, especially because the only requirement that I gave Sarah was simple: new construction. From flood damaged graduate residences to rundown, cockroach infested apartments to a trailer park mobile home, I had lived in some of the oldest, dirtiest, and problem-filled housings available. So, it was easy to justify my one request, regardless of the cost. I wanted to walk barefoot and feel comfortable lying on the carpet, not go to sleep feeling like I needed to wear a HAZMAT suit.

Job? Check. Apartment? Just about. Dog? Still searching.

To this day, I have found it crazy that people are so infatuated with purebreds and pedigrees. Now I will say that many new dog owners don't know what they're getting themselves into. And the same can be said for many self-proclaimed breeders, who breed first and worry about the genetics second. As a veterinarian, it doesn't take long to figure out whether the breeder is in it for the right reasons or to make a quick buck. Sure, everything in today's world revolves around money and perception, but even if an owner is financially comfortable or even wealthy, I feel that spending a couple thousand dollars on a dog is more often than not ridiculous and the epitome of materialism, especially when there are shelter dogs of all breeds begging for a home. Throw in the fact that their new pup's genetics and 'pure lineage' may be associated with big health problems and even bigger veterinary bills that can dwarf their initial purchase. But the more frequently people visit breeders and puppy mills, the more dogs they're going to pump out. The classic microeconomics concept of supply and demand is present even in the breeding world.

And this leads me to my bigger point. While I have nothing against breeders or purebred dogs, I can't help but think about how many shelter animals' lives could improve if they were as fortunate to share the benefits that their counterparts were lucky to have.

I recall when I searched online and entered my parent's zip code to unveil the pictures and descriptions for over 1,800 shelter dogs within a twenty-five mile radius. Think about that. One thousand, eight hundred dogs. That's when I knew that my search would include 'shelter dog.' And that confirmed my initial thoughts about the insanity behind spending big bucks on any purebred dog when hundreds of the abandoned remain confined in a 5'x5' cage for months, if not years, that is if they were to live that long.

It was a Wednesday night in June, and I just came home from another long day on the job. I'd been working there for only two weeks, but it felt like three months based on the length of the work day. My mom had made her pasta sauce for dinner, which didn't surprise me because Wednesday had always been associated with 'pasta night' for two decades. Ziti with ricotta cheese. Delicious, even more so since I had discovered that lunch hour only existed on my paper contract. Grabbing a plateful, I headed down to the man-cave, sat on the plaid couch, flipped on the Yankees, and picked up the 11th Hour

Shelter postcard that our neighbor Chris had given to me this past weekend. Let's start looking. I had always known the kind of dog I was looking for was a border-collie, Labrador retriever mix. So I did a search for these breeds on the website and pressed the 'Enter' key.

Up came a picture of a black and white colored dog.

Hello Oden, I smiled as I clicked on his newly discovered profile.

CHAPTER 5

Oden

"There's always another story. There's more than meets the eye."
— W.H. Auden, English poet

Meet n' Greet. That was the subject title of an email from Theresa, a volunteer at 11th Hour Shelter. I had sent an inquiry through the organization's website the night before last about arranging a time to meet Oden. The online pictures could not do this border collie mix justice, as his medium-length, sleek black coat, sickle tail, and joyous personality were portrayed in each image. *Boy, this search was easy,* I thought.

Along came Sunday afternoon. Little did I know that my drive up to Mount Olive later that week would become an all too familiar drive over the course of the next handful of weekends. It was yet another dreary day, with overcast skies and the occasional thunderstorm as I pulled into the shelter. *First time here, and hopefully the last,* I wished. The characteristic sights, sounds, and smells of a shelter were present in full force. I stepped out to the sight of two dogs in an outdoor pen and walked over to the fence to take a closer look at who was creating the commotion.

From the doorway approached a heavyset woman with a couple of leashes in her hands.

"Hi there! You must be Phil. I'm Maria," she stated as she extended her hand for a shake. "Sorry Theresa isn't able to make it, but she filled me in on your conversations." Her voice was being drowned out by those two dogs outside.

"Thor, quiet please," she pleaded, signaling for me to follow her. We headed into the outdoor run in an attempt to quiet the upheaval. I'm sure the sight of the leash did not help calm his excitement any. Thor, a muscular grey pitbull terrier, continued to bark and chose not to repress his vocal vitality. Not surprising. Gosh, twenty seconds of this cacophony made me realize he had a zero percent chance of ever setting foot into our apartment.

The other dog stood quietly to his left, with the only noise being made by the constant wave of his tail. His upright posture and proper demeanor was a refreshing contrary to his counterpart. His ribs were visible to the naked eye, yet despite that, I knew his weight was still too much. *Wish he was a bit smaller,* I said to myself, keeping in mind the thirty-five pound limit hanging over my head.

As my eyes made contact with his, it was as if that released his inner excitement, and he lunged forward, planting his white front paws on my chest, leaving behind an imprint of each on my once white t-shirt.

"Down Miles," Maria instructed, as she stepped in between us. "Sorry about that, he's just excited."

We left the outdoor run, leaving behind yin and yang, and proceeded to enter the back entrance to the shelter. Upon opening the door, the noise of dozens of dogs reverberated throughout, reminding me of the days of my first job as a kennel worker at the veterinary hospital down the road from my childhood home. I recalled being inside the hospital kennel in the early morning hours and how I was surrounded by complete silence, but as soon as a bag of food was opened, a bowl was clanged, or a door swung ajar, I knew too well that a deafening sound was in the immediate future. I don't miss those days. Cleaning up poop for $7.00 an hour stunk. Taking crap as a fourteen-year-old kennel boy made it even worse. Good thing those were distant memories as my thoughts transitioned back to meeting Oden.

Once inside the shelter, we walked around the cages and took a look at other dogs as the kennel crew remained hard at work. The site of filling up water and food bowls, refilling spray bottles and repeatedly dumping the mop buckets rekindled the thoughts. The characteristic smell of crap mixed with bleach emanated wherever we headed, which triggered those old pesky recollections from my time as a kennel attendant. Not a good thing.

"Now I know you're here to see Oden," Maria started. "But I just want to say that I don't think that is a good idea."

"Oden?" a voice chirped in from in front of the sink. "Yeah, I wouldn't even bring him out here," shouted a volunteer as she placed the washed dishes on drying racks.

Biting my tongue, all I could think was what the hell was going on. I came here to see this dog. The dog's pictures were on the website, so he was clearly available for adoption. My email from two days earlier did not give any indication that Oden was not going to be there. Was he adopted? His pictures and online video seemed like the happy, obedient dog playing fetch that I always wanted. It was like a sinking feeling. And who was this lady Maria to tell me that *she* didn't think that it was a good idea?

"Oden has had five different foster families, but unfortunately he's been returned. In fact, I fostered him most recently but he's a special dog that needs to have just one person in the home with him," Maria continued.

"Why was he returned?" I pressed her. "Five times!" I felt like I deserved to know.

"He bit someone in each of the foster family houses," showing me her hand. "He was doing fine for the first couple of days at my house, but he became territorial. He'd probably do best in a quiet home, perhaps with an older individual who would be devoted to training him."

Hell with that. I wasn't going to be bringing a dog like that home. I could just see how that conversation was going to go. 'Hey Sarah, meet Oden, he likes to play fetch and tug of war, especially with your wrist...'

I was actually surprised that he was given so many chances. It's not like he was returned because he wasn't house-broken. Five chances is a lot. In fact, I was surprised he wasn't given the pink juice instead of a sixth chance.

For the individuals supporting animal rights groups, don't take that the wrong way. Imagine if instead of biting a hand of a forty-year-old woman, it was the face of your four-year-old child.

Changes your perspective, huh?

"Yeah, I don't need that." Talk about doing a 180 degree switch. The thought of seeing Oden went out of my mind. No need to go down that route. Nonetheless, it was still a disappointment. The looks of a border collie and the energy of a border collie were there, but the polarizing behavior was synonymous with a junk yard Rottweiler. Having a dog should be a pleasure, not a nerve-racking, fearful experience.

"We have lots of other dogs here, like Rocko," pointing to the corner near the entrance. A medium-size, brown, short-haired mix cowered in the far end of his crate. "He's been here for a few weeks, came from Georgia."

Within two seconds, another volunteer brought a dog through the back door on a leash. But what was not on a leash was Rocko's temperament, as his aggression was unleashed like a slingshot. His lips curled, revealing his white canines eager to sink into a piece of flesh. The hackles became erect as he lunged forward, pressing his muzzle through the top side of the cage. The center latch on this flimsy crate was being pushed to its limits.

Maria raced to the crate and put her hands against the door to prevent Rocko from advancing and getting his neck stuck in between the cage and the door. Rocko's booming bark continued as his gaze focused on the passing white dog instead of Maria's fingers.

Holy crap, I mumbled, laughing nervously to myself. *What was going on here?*

"Let's go upstairs where it's quieter. We can talk about what you're looking for." Maria led me outside, across the lot, and up to the office area. She motioned for me to have a seat on the sofa as she pulled up a folding chair.

"I want a dog that has a personality. I don't want to take the dog out of the dog," I recall informing her.

We went back and forth for a couple of minutes. Breed of dog. Energy. Age. She asked an assistant in the room to bring in Riley.

"I think he's going to like her," she confided to her friend.

A couple of minutes later, a tan, medium coat, hound-Doberman mix entered the room. Obedient. Leash-trained. Responsive. Happy.

"Wow, what a great looking dog," I nodded as Riley raised her right paw onto my open hand. Smart too.

The only thing missing was that internal gut feeling that I just didn't have, at least not at that time. I was set in my mind on the type of dog I wanted. I always told myself to use my head when thinking about something, but to follow my gut instinct when it comes to actually making that decision. Riley was a nice dog, but on that Sunday afternoon, I just wasn't feeling it.

"Has anyone else come to look at Riley?" I questioned Maria, gauging the possible interest from other suitors. I didn't want to look back in a couple of days and learn that she was in someone else's home. My insides were starting to churn because I wanted a dog, but I didn't want to settle just to have one.

"No one yet. She just arrived earlier this week, but you never know who may come in through that door," Maria replied.

I grew restless in my seat and was looking for an escape route. I went on to thank Maria for the time, telling her, "I think I'm going to think about this a bit longer."

I knew that wasn't the case. I didn't need to.

The clouds had darkened outside, and the cool rain dripped down the back of my neck as I headed across the parking lot. I left with a headache so the water felt good on my head. I plopped down into my driver's side seat and reached for my cell phone on the console.

Three text messages, one missed call. I phoned Sarah immediately.

"How'd it go? How's Oden" I heard on the other end of the line.

"Heh, I don't know," I laughed as I started to tell Sarah about Oden's history. "I can't believe the description on the web page read, 'Gentle, Affectionate, Good with adults.'" Given Oden's track record, man, I'd hate to see one of the shelter's dogs that wasn't labeled gentle, affectionate, or good with adults.

I didn't mention Riley. And that was not intentional. In fact, I didn't even think about telling Sarah about her. Instead, we talked about Sarah's mother's upcoming birthday. She wanted me to come up to Connecticut to have a family dinner next weekend. She floated the idea of spending the afternoon at the beach, and then barbequing some chicken and steaks that night. 'Uh huh, yeah, okay, alright. Sounds good to me.' That was the extent of my responses on my drive back to my parents' home. I could only think about that one happy dog I met earlier in the afternoon. *What was his name again,* I pondered.

Oh yeah, Miles.

CHAPTER 6

The Fourth of July

"Instinct is a marvelous thing. It can neither be explained nor ignored."
— Agatha Christie, author of *The Mysterious Affair at Styles*

July 7, 2013.

Another weekend. Another Sunday. And yet another trip up to Mount Olive, New Jersey for a pet adoption event. This time I was heading to the PetSmart rather than the shelter itself.

I woke up early on Sunday morning on the Fourth of July weekend to continue the search for man's best friend. I stayed up late the night before to scroll through images and read the profiles on the Eleventh Hour Shelter website. Sarah had sent me an email with a link to a few profiles, but nothing that really caught my attention. In fact, it seemed like she didn't get my memo.

If I said I wanted a black Labrador, Sarah would send me a picture of a white pit bull. If I desired to have a young dog, she'd ask me to look at the profile of Lucy, an 8-year old pointer. If I preferred a medium to large sized breed, she'd suggest Snoopy, a beagle. At first I figured this was unintentional, but I eventually came to the conclusion that her goal was to broaden my horizon and to be open minded. I always smiled when I opened the links. For one, I knew they were going to be the polar opposite of what I was looking for. And two, the subject line in her email would always read 'Sooo cute!' or 'I want, I want!'

Sarah was planning to head down from Connecticut to New Jersey by the early afternoon. She too worked late last night and decided to sleep at home in her own bed. But I didn't want to miss out on the event and show up after dozens of people already scoured the area before I would get there. First come, first served.

As I walked through the sliding doors at 9 am, I could see that there was a designated area in the back of the store where the adoption event was taking place. There were a couple of volunteers behind a booth with the organization's banner clearly displayed above them. Well at least I was at the right place. A large room was being used to hold some of the 'resident' dogs while outside the doorway there were cages with about ten other dogs of various breeds arranged in a semi-circle. *They must have transported them in from the shelter this morning,* I thought as I walked by them.

The place was already a zoo, no pun intended. Kids were running around while parents were in pursuit. A choir of barking was echoing throughout. What else could I expect, right?

The plan was to have a Meet n' Greet with Lily, an 8-month-old Border Collie mix. It wasn't a scheduled session so that's why I wanted to be early. Nevertheless, I wasn't thrilled with the idea of having a puppy. I couldn't see myself potty-training or giving one the around the clock attention it needed. Having said that, Lily's profile kept me intrigued. Plus, I was holding out hope that she was older than what was actually listed. With this in mind, I approached the booth.

"Good morning, how may I help you?" questioned the volunteer, who was wearing the characteristic black and gold 11th Hour Shelter t-shirt.

After a short discussion, I was led towards the observation area. En route we bypassed a handful of cages, some of which were filled with puppies and others with solo occupants. We headed down the hallway and entered the designated space, essentially an empty room with a bench. I signed a waiver allowing me to interact with Lily, this vicious 8-month-old puppy. Nowadays, even shelters have to cover themselves in case something goes wrong. To their defense, I wouldn't want to be responsible either if a dog that had only been in the shelter for a couple of days and was relatively unknown randomly bit someone.

I paced around the cement floor before choosing to sit on the wooden bench. The feeling of isolation from my surroundings began to sink in. I couldn't imagine what these shelter animals were feeling. Bouncing around from one location to the next. Day in and day out. Sleepless nights. The only sensation is the cold feeling from the cement floors. For many, hope had been replaced with despair. The sadness of the past, insecurity of the moment and the uncertainty of tomorrow could only be replaced by the longing for a better day.

My thoughts were interrupted by the opening of the door.

"She's shy," the volunteer smiled as she tugged the leash, inching Lily forward. She paused before placing her paw in front of the next. Her apprehension was palpable as the door closed behind her.

Eight months? No way. Maybe six, I thought. I squatted down on the floor and began to call her name.

Nothing. Not even a recognition, tilt of the head, or perk of the ears. She just remained frozen in the corner, hoping that if she didn't move a muscle that I wouldn't be able to see her black frame outlined against the white background of the wall. I went over to her and reached out my hand to her muzzle. I got a few sniffs but that was it. This was a lackluster interaction that I did not anticipate coming, especially with a puppy. Yes, she was still young and probably didn't even know her name, but as is the case with any interaction, you want a connection. Better to try and figure out if it's the right fit now rather than in a few hours at home after the papers have been signed. Adopting a dog is like a novel fisherman going out on the water for the first time. A few minutes on the water can feel like an eternity, and if there isn't any action initially, one can be eager to recast the fishing line, perhaps a little bit too soon.

But sometimes you just need to follow your gut instinct.

I waited for the volunteer to re-enter the room. The ten minute interaction was nine minutes too long. My hesitancies of having a puppy were rekindled within the first moments.

I politely thanked her for her time. My innuendo that Lily was not the right choice was understood. We walked down the hall towards the play pen where I asked if I could walk around the back area where other dogs in cages filled the closed-off room. Plenty of prospective adopters were mingling amongst their suitors.

The rarities of a three legged Pointer and a one-eyed Cockapoo were bright and center in the middle of the room. Their note cards on the front of the cages gave information about their past, or at least what sounded good on paper.

For most shelter dogs, this is their last chance at life, so the words written on an index card are meticulously chosen to describe what someone may feel to be the best dog ever. If you have never been to a shelter, you'll have to trust me or go take a look for yourself. Words matter, including those about a dog's age. If there is any uncertainty about how old he is, more often than not the shelter's best estimate will be that he is two years old. For the most part, potential owners do not want to take in a dog that's already deemed, rightly or wrongly, 'too old' or even have the financial burden of health issues more likely to impact an older dog. On the opposite end of the spectrum, many of those searching for their potential addition want to make sure the dog is not too young where crate and potty training are more than just occasional inconveniences but daily problems. For the most part, people want the idea of having a dog to be easy. Truthfully, many soon-to-be pet owners do not want to come home after work at 7 pm to have another job in training a new pet or managing the problems every night. It's the shelter's job to do their best to alleviate those concerns, at least until they get home with Fido.

That was enough for today as I headed out into the PetSmart lobby. Walking past the booth I thanked the staff for their time, knowing that today was not the day. The same two dogs that were barking when I arrived were still going at it. Jeez. *Do you guys not want to be adopted?* Deciding that it was best not to get in the middle of that back and forth interaction, I headed in the opposite direction where out of the corner of my eye, the contrast of a white tip on a black tail caught my attention.

"Miles?" I muttered with a curious expression on my face as I turned back to read his cage card.

Go figure.

Thump, thump. Miles wagged his tail against the bottom of his crate. His chest was projected out and his head was held high. There he was, just like last time, laying quietly amongst the cacophony in his surroundings while remaining alert amid the commotion in the environs of yet another adoption event.

I couldn't believe it. I wasn't even expecting him to be there. In fact, I was surprised that he wasn't laying down in someone's kitchen or on a living room sofa by now.

And that's when it hit me. I didn't need to look for a dog anymore. He was staring right at me.

Sarah had just crossed the Tappan Zee Bridge when she answered my phone call.

"Hey Phil, so how was..."

"...Sarah, I found our dog," I expressed, cutting her off. Sarah responded with a rhetorical question, but I glanced over it. I was too excited to tell her of my decision.

"You'll never believe who I ran into." Without giving her the chance to respond, I told her about Miles.

"What is the likelihood," I commented. "Come on, I see this dog two weeks in a row, and by chance I just so happen to run into him while leaving yet another adoption event. It's like an omen."

The idea that I could lose the opportunity to have this dog bothered me. It would really eat at me if I passed up on Miles, and he went to another home. I didn't want to settle and have just any dog. I knew what I was looking for and this was it. From the looks to the personality to the age, he was the rescue mutt that I longed for. If I were asked when I was ten years old to describe my ideal dog, this was what I had always envisioned. I didn't want the opportunity to pass by. With that in mind, I couldn't let another week or two go by as my search continued. The hypothetical emptiness that I feared would fill my insides if someone else came in and scooped him up would bother me for years. I wouldn't be able to let it go. And this was the thought process I had about a lot of things in my life. Live with no regrets.

The roads were crowded on this Fourth of July as I headed back to my parents' home. Even in the late morning hours, the sun was out in full force as I stepped out into the driveway. The expected summer humidity wasn't helping any as I headed over to the porch, where my dad was watering the hanging flower baskets. To this day, salmon-colored Impatiens have been my mom's favorite flower and every year it remains my dad's responsibility to take care of them.

"They don't look like the neighbors' flowers," I joked, pointing to the flourishing array of botanical beauty across the street. The bright blue hydrangeas, pink begonias and multi-colored day lilies were an array of contrast, literally and figuratively.

"You better watch it," he responded, playfully raising his clenched fist to my chin. Taking a jab at my dad's flowers was like a body blow to his outdoor gardening credibility. But in all fairness, their usual summer arrangement of Impatiens or petunias baked in the sunshine all day. Given their location in the open front porch, all the fertilizer and water couldn't replace the most important component that lacked: shade. My dad knew this, but every year, the same flower appeared in the same basket. And my mom would be the first to let him know that despite his hard work, the neighbor's flowers looked great.

We laughed as we exchanged our wisecrack pleasantries. Our talk then transitioned to the morning adoption event and whether 'Lady Sarah,' as my dad says to this day, would be coming for breakfast.

Sarah would be arriving shortly, and I didn't want to go inside yet. It was only a little after ten o'clock, and I knew all too well that my mom wouldn't even be downstairs yet for breakfast. With her aging physique and long, drawn-out morning routine, a family breakfast wouldn't start until lunch time in the Casale household. Knowing that, I elected to stay outside and pass the time. I strolled up the street to the walking path that ran the length of the housing development. The cover from the oak trees provided me a safe haven from the sun's rays, but was of little help from the still air and oppressive humidity that engulfed me. I could feel the sweat beads slowly drip down the center of my back. Typical New Jersey summertime weather accompanied me on my walk along the pathway.

It was late morning and I had a lot to think about. My mind had been racing for quite some time. For one, my mom's health was unfortunately in a decline, and two, it was my dad who was having an increased role with increased expectations. Working two full-time jobs, one in the corporate world and one at home, seemed to be taking its toll on him. Project manager by day and homemaker by night. The plan was to retire in the upcoming year, downsize, and move south, away from the land of high property taxes, but with medical expenses piling up, the perfect storm was brewing on the horizon. So much for the golden years, right?

With my parents on my mind, I looked forward to the simple things to take my mind off of everyday reality. As was the case through veterinary school, my online video chat conversations with Sarah remained the thrill of the day. Using it allowed us to have e-conversations on important topics like the Yankees,

Monday night football, politics, and sometimes the less essential things like our apartment hunt.

A golden Retriever rushed forward in my direction on the path, pulling his owner by the leash. It was Mr. Taylor, one of my parents' longtime neighbors down the block. He threw his arm in the air while shaking his head, acknowledging the common everyday occurrences of the morning walk routine.

"Who's walking whom," I smiled.

"This was supposed to be the kids' job," he chuckled. Too bad his kids were young adults heading off to college in a couple of months.

The sight of the retriever halted my thoughts about my family and pivoted my thinking towards my future dog. At that time in my life, the search for a dog was my escape. Sure, I loved talking with Sarah, and I couldn't wait to get home to chat with her as the topics like work, apartments, and dogs came up in past weeks. Even if I came home from my job late at night, the search for an apartment and now, a furry friend, helped me get through the day. Not to dwell on my job, but there were red flags already, ranging from the extended, unpaid hours to staffing inadequacies. I needed to have something to look forward to, and it was worth exploring, even at ten o'clock at night.

Beep beep. The car horn belonged to a passing dark navy Subaru Legacy. Sarah was here. *Breakfast time*, I thought, as I headed back home.

"Sarah, I found our dog!" I reiterated, giving her a bear hug. "We have to write an email right away, I don't want to lose this chance." We went inside to find the usual weekend display of a filleted fruit platter, prepared by, of course, my father.

"Lady Sarah's here," he exclaimed, clapping his hands together. It was great to see the 'breath of fresh air' that my best friend infused into my dad's lungs. Those were his words.

We sat down for a family breakfast, where my mom generously offered Sarah one of each: crumb cake, pastries, Kaiser rolls, scones, did I mention crumb cake?

"I bought them for you, sweetie," she said. I looked up at my dad with a sly eye. We laughed.

We conversed about the usual standard topics like Sarah's work, sports, even the dog search, paying careful attention to avoid my mom's health. Way too negative and depressing for a Sunday, especially on a holiday weekend.

After breakfast, Sarah and I sat down on the basement couch and wrote an email to the rescue group to arrange a meeting with Miles. I would check my email hourly after that to see if there was a response, up until the time we left for fireworks. There wasn't one.

It was around 7:30 at night when we all packed into mom's Caravan and headed over to the parking lot at the local grocery store to watch fireworks. Located in the town just down the road from our prospective apartment, we thought this would be a good spot to watch the celebration. Undoubtedly, it would be less crowded than the park up the road where they were going to be launched. It took us only twenty minutes to get there, the norm for that drive down Route 202. The lot was crowded, but we found a place to set up camp. I guess a lot of other people had the same idea as us. So much for a novel idea. We arranged our lawn chairs in a semi-circle, cracked open a few drinks, and tossed the ball around until the fading sun set below the hills in the west. Shortly after nine o'clock, the sky filled with a display of symbolic colors and the characteristic pops and crackles we grew to expect on this holiday.

"What a show," my mom remarked as my dad placed his arm over her shoulder. After nearly forty years of marriage, it was nice to see their devotion.

People were whooping and hollering as dozens of fireworks filled the night sky. All types of fireworks were on display. From the chrysanthemum fireworks with their distinctive long trailers to the spherical shape of the round shell explosions, the dark night lit up for nearly a half hour. When the grand finale ended, the stillness filled the air, leaving behind the metallic smell of smoke. It was a nice night up until then, but chaos ensued as thousands of people began to leave the poorly designed parking lot through the same exit. We waited in gridlock as cars inched forward amongst the sound of horns and a choice selection of vocabulary from their drivers. That continued for nearly two hours. It was a little before midnight when we got home.

"Two hours! Never again," I told Sarah as we walked through the garage door into the house. "Next time I'm watching the Macy's fireworks...from home." I opened up my laptop and waited for about five minutes for the antiquated computer to load. Eventually, I logged into my email.

One new message.

CHAPTER 7

The Meeting

*"A stunning first impression was not the
same thing as love at first sight.
But surely it was an invitation to consider the matter."*
— Lois McMaster Bujold, author

"Are you excited?" Sarah asked, knowing all too well that I was jumping out of my socks.

We were on our way to finally go meet Miles one-on-one. It was hard to believe. And as the anticipation grew within, I couldn't help but think how it all transpired over the past week.

When we returned home from the aforementioned fireworks spectacle the previous weekend, I had received an email from Maggie, a volunteer with Eleventh Hour Shelter. I learned that this fifth grade teacher had been fostering Miles in her house for the past two weeks. Fortunately for Miles, school was out for summer recess, and Maggie had opened up her doors to him. Almost like a vacation from the penitentiary of confinement. That brought a smile to my face. Some positive news for a change that I'm sure he welcomed. I figured anything would beat the daily sight of concrete floors and wire cages.

We arranged to meet the following Sunday at Mount Olive Dog Park in North Jersey. Over the week, she sent me a couple emails telling me about Miles and what he was doing at their house. It was almost like she was making a sales pitch by telling me about all of his positive traits. His happiness. His personality. His disciplined behavior. Paraphrasing, she even noted that "he only barked once when he saw a bird on the deck."

Little did we know.

It was a quiet Sunday morning with the dew still present on the tips of the grass blades as we pulled into the park. The dog park was located in the back corner surrounded by a few thirty-foot tall oak trees. The faint morning breeze from the southwest was refreshing as we headed over towards the double gated entrance of the fenced-in park. That same wind would be bringing the heat and humidity later in the day, so it was easy to enjoy the refreshing seventy degree start to the morning.

A white Chevy Trailblazer was parked in front of the entrance. "I wonder if that's them?" Sarah asked.

At that moment, a tall brunette in her late 30s wearing a short sleeve shirt and shorts got out of the car and opened the hatchback on her SUV. Out sprung that familiar black coated, white tailed dog who would not stop jumping towards her hand in an attempt to steal the leash.

"Phil?" she asked, extending her hand. "Hi, I'm Maggie and this is Miles..."

Boom. He plunged his front paws into my belly, unexpectedly knocking the wind out from me and predictably drawing a smirk from Sarah.

"Sorry about that," Maggie pronounced, handing over Sarah the reigns. "Why don't we take him inside," she suggested, pointing to the dog park before pulling her hair back into a bun. "He'll like to see his friends."

Once inside the enclosure, Miles began to walk around the perimeter, hesitant to leave the side of Maggie. I couldn't blame him. She feeds him, walks him, gives him a home. I wouldn't want to step away from the source that gives me a life.

"It's okay Miles, go ahead," she implored. He would take a few steps away then come back to her side. I could see his hesitancy to not go too far. At the same time I could feel his desire to run free. Within a couple minutes, the space between them went from a couple feet to a few yards. But he would continue to run back, yearning for the attention which I could only assume that he had been deprived of in recent months.

RUFF, RUFF, Ruff, Ruff, ruff. A short-haired Dachshund came racing over from the nearby picnic tables where a couple of owners were chatting. He made his presence known to all of us. That included Miles, who squatted down on all fours low to the ground, his muzzle nearly touching the blades of grass. He was ready to pounce, and with that, he was off. Seemingly forgetting where he was and who he was with, Miles exploded from the starting line. The game of tag had begun, and he was in full pursuit as he darted after his new acquaintance. Miles' gracefulness was clearly apparent as he galloped around the park, almost like he was effortlessly floating across the ground. His stride was so smooth, as if he had perfected it in the farmlands of the Kentucky fields where I could picture him herding sheep and cattle flawlessly.

We headed over to the picnic tables, where shortly after, Maggie caught his attention. He trotted over, his open mouth revealing his white teeth as he nuzzled his nose under her arm. His fondness for Maggie was undeniable, but short-lived as the Dachshund approached again. And just like that, the zigzagging pursuit ensued for another round.

"Miles! Come here!" Maggie implored. "I want him to interact with you guys too."

"It's okay, he's having fun," Sarah remarked, but that didn't stop Maggie from heading over to the tables to try and reel in Miles. Good luck.

He evaded her for a few seconds as he grew increasingly distracted by the dozen or so dogs and people interacting in the area. His white tipped tail, upright in position, helped us follow him from afar. Weaving in between and around other dogs, Miles came to a stop at a water bowl. As he lapped up the water, Maggie seized the opportunity and clipped on his leash. Party's over, he realized. Bummer.

As we met up with the four legged renegade, Maggie handed us his leash and told us to "go have fun" with him. "I'll be over here when you're ready," she said, pointing to the adjacent social gathering of dog owners.

We walked to the other end of the park. At first Miles was hesitant, looking back every handful of steps to check if Maggie was there. While the distance grew between them, so did the variety of the park's sights and smells. New trees, new bushes. Miles barely lifted his head as he pulled Sarah along, sniffing everything along his path. A park bench in a mulch bed was a big hit in the distance. I didn't think it had anything to do with the vibrant color, but the fact that it was probably the main attraction in the park. We steered clear of that and headed along the perimeter fencing, which I didn't think was a much better option, for I was all but certain that every inch of it was one day or another saturated with different dogs' bodily fluids at some point.

"Remember what I told you about getting a dog," I asked Sarah as we methodically moved along the fenced boundaries of the park. That was my chance to remind her of the keys to adopting the dog with the right behavior. There were a couple simple ways to figure out a dog's temperament. For one, being able to take his food bowl away without him growling is an important step. If you can't get near his bowl, forget it. Your hand will be his next meal. And two, if you can, put your hands in the jowls of his mouth to see what his reaction is. Of course this is easier said than done. But with all honesty, the last thing anyone needs is an aggressive dog. Sarah was well aware of that. From what I could tell from that brief visit and our previous interactions, Miles was anything but aggressive.

Our pace picked up as we circled back to the picnic area. The visualization and sounds of barking dogs drew Miles' focus as we approached Maggie. We chatted for a couple more minutes before heading towards our cars. The play date was over.

"What do you think Miles?" Maggie questioned playfully, holding her hands out to her sides. "Did you have fun?"

And at that moment his tail stopped wagging. He dropped to the sidewalk and rolled on his back, exposing his white belly for a submissive rub at which Sarah graciously obliged. I remember standing there smiling, almost needing to pinch myself to see if this had been a dream.

No, it was reality. Even better.

"Let's say that we choose to take in Miles. What do we do from here? Do we speak with you?" I asked.

Maggie explained that if we decide to proceed, then she will reach out to her superior, Tina, and arrange for Miles to be at the Mount Olive Kennel the day before we take him home.

Nodding my head, I told Maggie we would be in touch with her by the end of the day. And with that, we said our goodbyes and watched as Miles pranced away down the sidewalk before jumping into the cargo area of that Chevy Blazer.

That got me thinking. *I wonder how he's going to like the backseat of my Hyundai Accent.*

CHAPTER 8

A TRIP TO THE VET

*"Dogs feel very strongly that they should always go
with you in the car, in case the need should arise for
them to bark violently at nothing right in your ear."*
— Dave Barry, Pulitzer Prize winning American author

"Who wants to go to the park?"

Those words never seemed to go unanswered. Whether chewing on a peanut butter stuffed Kong or in an apparent deep sleep, everything else would become second as he sprung to life. Literally. It was almost expected that his front paws would be implanted on your chest within seconds if you even whispered those words.

2013. It was the first week in September, and yes, we were off to the park. At that point, we had Miles only for couple of days, so we were still figuring him out. I guess it's fair to say that feeling was mutual.

Take for example the drive to Duke Island Park. Every time Miles heard the clicking sound of the car turn signal as we veered onto Old York Road, it was as if he knew where we were going. He would start to whimper and pace around the back seat of my car. I would see his head moving back and forth in the rear view mirror. To the left, then to the right, then back to the left. I would hear his panting in the background. At some point, I would occasionally feel the claws of his right paw on my shoulder, and I would know all too well that those gouge marks would last a week. Having said that, the worst part was the inevitable yelp that would rattle anyone's frame of mind. Though I would anticipate it, it would rarely help. I would usually be on my phone or listening to sports talk radio, all while focusing on driving when Miles forgotten presence would be rekindled by the sound of his bark. His high pitch yap would cause my ears to ring because more often than not, it was about six inches from my right ear.

So on that September morning when Sarah and I took Miles to the park for the first time ever, I learned the hard way. I laugh as I write this, but that late summer drive on that road scared the hell out of me. Little did I know there would be bigger things to worry about that morning.

To make a long story short, we took Miles for a stroll around the paved walking path in the park, when he decided it was time to go to the bathroom. When I saw some white things coiling back and forth in his stool, I knew our next stop that morning would be at the veterinary hospital I worked at.

Tapeworms, or any intestinal parasite for that matter, can be somewhat mundane to a veterinarian. I ran about ten fecal exams a day a work so looking at this stuff was ho hum. But when it's your dog with those things inside of him, the mindset can quickly change.

For Miles, I wasn't too surprised. A dog with a limited medical history, that was abandoned in Kentucky, and bounced around different crowded shelters was bound to have something festering in his intestinal tract. I was more concerned with the fact that he might have fleas. Tapeworms can come from a dog ingesting a flea that carries the larvae, and the last thing I needed was for my undercover dog to be the source of an infestation in our new apartment.

"Fleas can lay forty to fifty eggs a day," I informed Sarah. That's the concern there, as I jokingly looked at her clothes. I didn't think Miles had fleas, but I didn't want to chance it.

The last place I wanted to go on my day off was work. I already spent upwards of fifty plus hours there a week. I had no desire to spend a single minute more, but I knew what needed to be done. I called my colleague Dr. Seacrest to see if she would just take a look at him. I'm legally not allowed to treat my own dog, otherwise, I would have been practicing some back-alley medicine.

When we arrived, the easiest part at the veterinary hospital was checking in. Then the shit hit the fan, no pun intended.

Miles needed an injection of Praziquantel to treat his tapeworms. All you need to know about this drug is the following: Imagine having a cut on your finger and submerging it in 70% isopropyl alcohol. That's exactly what it feels like when Praziquantel is injected underneath the skin. There's a bit of a delayed reaction, and by bit, I mean a few seconds. Being a new graduate out of school, I knew what drug to use, how to dose it, where to give it, but I learned that afternoon that you better have a good restraint on the pet being administered it.

Within two seconds of that subcutaneous injection, Miles threw me around like a ragdoll on the raised metal exam room table as I struggled to wrangle this creature that just so happened to be...my dog? *What the hell*, I remarked nervously as I held on for the ride. My face turned red as Miles dragged me from one edge of the exam table to the other. He eventually jumped off and started to squeal bloody murder as he tried to bite at his back, the area where the injection was administered.

"It was Dr. Seacrest, not me," I said, pointing at the lady in the white coat. *Maybe we should have given him the vaccines first,* I wondered.

A similar battle ensued, and that was just for my attempt to restrain him again, let alone the response to getting poked with a needle for his inoculations.

"We're done Miles, we're done! Good boy, what a good boy," Dr. Seacreast remarked, rubbing behind his ears.

No, we weren't. Little did she know that I wanted to trim his nails.

Anyone that has ever tried to cut their own dog's nails at home knows how difficult it can be. From the endless rounds of the wrestling match to the delicacy of avoiding the quick, or blood supply, when trimming the nails, it's a lot easier to pay someone fifteen bucks for that pedicure than it is to clean the blood stains out of your carpet following the ordeal.

Having said that, Miles nail trim went about as well as if we had trimmed them at our apartment by ourselves. When we tried to get him to lay on his side, all he started to do was resist us. I wasn't shocked by that, figuring we had just gone through two rounds in our previous tussle. We were sweating. He was wound up, panting non-stop as the pale skin near the base of his nose turned bright red. He was starting to get nippy, so he earned himself a party hat. As we came up with a plan to restrain him, it made me chuckle when I saw Miles continue to outsmart us. In his latest Houdini attempt, every time anyone would touch him, he would drop to the ground and start to roll like an alligator. Yes, our dog was alligator rolling. When two of us finally pinned him down, his only other option was to start peeing. We would move him along the ground to another area of the floor, and as soon as one of his paws was touched, he let loose. One muzzle. Two restrainers. Ten minutes. Zero nail bleeds. Yes, that's worth fifteen bucks, don't you think?

I took care of the bill. No one was more excited to get out of there, to explore a new place and see what new smells could be discovered elsewhere than Miles. And with that, he tugged forward on the leash, leading us outside to that Indian summer heat.

"Stressful day for little buddy, huh?" Sarah claimed as she opened the door to the back seat.

Little did we know how much that morning took out of him. As we came to a halt at the first red light, I glanced at the back seat and saw Miles taking his afternoon nap a little earlier than expected.

CHAPTER 9

Jail Break

"There is no faith which has never yet been broken except that of a truly faithful dog."
— Konrad Lorenz, Austrian zoologist

Our apartment complex had a small fitness center located in the clubhouse, right next to the leasing center. It was open from 5:30 in the morning, so as an early bird, I would roll out of bed and head over before going to work. While I did have a membership at the local gym down the road, I sometimes chose to go to the apartment gym on those rainy mornings or when I wanted to sleep in for an extra twenty minutes. In the first winter at our new apartment, I quickly realized that by the time my car warmed up, I could have already walked to and from the apartment fitness center.

It was an early Saturday morning in late September 2013. I could hear the rain pounding the rooftops of the cars in the parking lot outside of our bedroom window. The thought of staying in bed or watching the morning news crossed my mind, but I finally decided that I would get a quick workout in instead.

We had Miles now for a couple of weeks, but I was still hesitant to leave him alone. Sarah was working her overnight nursing shift at the medical center so I didn't have anyone to watch over him when I left. Knowing that Miles would bark if I put him in his crate, a no-no for the 6 am hour, I thought, *why not just put him in the second bedroom?* Sounds reasonable and considerate, doesn't it? To cut to the chase, I left Miles in that empty room. I figured he would have a window to look out of and soft carpet to lie down on for the next thirty minutes. Well, I was clearly wrong. When I came back I found the blinds covering the two windows crinkled and bent, but fortunately still functional. I couldn't believe it. He must have been jumping at the window the entire time...

I had just made my first mistake by thinking Miles was going to be like every other dog. My second mistake was thinking he would change.

A couple nights later, Sarah texted me saying she was off to work. She was planning on leaving Miles outside his crate in the living room. I remember telling her that I didn't think it was a good idea. She disagreed and texted me, 'He'll be fine.' Well when I came home, I walked into a disaster site. The wood floors were scratched, probably from him racing around them like a crazed animal. Add that to the security deposit deduction. The oak coat rack was pulled down, which caused the pegs to break off. Sarah's coat and purse, which hung from those pegs when I left in the morning, were punctured and ripped apart. Highlighters and pens were burst over the carpet, which left blotches of ink saturated in the rug in different patterns. The couch pillow was torn wide open, its insides scattered around the room. I took out my antiquated flip phone and took a picture to send to Sarah, but that image wouldn't do justice nor would my choice of words that followed. The room looked like it had been ransacked.

After the initial shell shock, I began to clean up the room. Thank God for carpet cleaner. With one eye on Miles, I started working on the carpets. This was the last thing I wanted to do at 8 o'clock at night. And the whole time I repeatedly asked Miles, "What are we going to do with you?" Speaking of our trouble maker, he seemed unfazed by the whole situation as he continued to wag his tail while he watched me clean up the mess.

That night, however, brought about changes for our furry friend.

Forget damaging the apartment or losing the security deposit, I was worried that Miles would get into something he wasn't supposed to. Yeah, that may be my veterinarian's mindset, but losing my dog or dropping $3,000 on a foreign body surgery or hospital ICU stay wasn't in my plans. From that point on, I decided that Miles' new home was going to be his crate when we were not there.

Miles' separation anxiety was indescribable. The smallest things like sitting out on the porch would make him go crazy. Even when Sarah and I took a sixty second stroll to the mailbox, Miles would begin to race around the apartment from the main entrance door to the sliding door window. His nerves would trigger his relentless barking, which would cause that same pale, furless blotch of skin by his nose to light up red. And when we came in, he would jump on us as if he hadn't seen us in months. "Miles, it's only been a minute," Sarah would say as she attempted to comfort him upon entering the apartment.

We would soon be reminded of the ramifications of his anxiety.

It was a Friday night in November 2013. Sarah had gone through her new normal routine of getting herself and Miles ready for a work night. It was just like every other time for the past two months, or so it seemed.

Miles' crate was located in the hall connecting the master bedroom with the bathroom. We placed a light brown quilt over the top, leaving the entrance door to the crate uncovered. Our hopes were that the comforter would not only suppress the sound of his barking, but create a dark environment to encourage him to take a nap. We placed a fan in front and played some music in the background. We wanted to keep him calm, cool, and collected. Or so we had intended.

Reluctant to go into his cage, Sarah would have to lure him in with his dinner. No, we couldn't leave him with a bowl of food or water because he would end up chewing the stainless steel sides or rubber rimmed bottom when no one was around. Instead, she would dump one and half cups of kibble along the cage bottom and lock the door after he entered. It was their nightly routine performed right before she left for work around 6 pm.

I was scheduled to work until 7:00 at night, but with my job, I never left on time. On many nights, I would be lucky to get out by 7:30, and as the years went by, that often expanded by another hour. But one thing that wouldn't change would be my nightly routine when I pulled into the apartment complex after work. When I stepped out of my car in front of our apartment, I would always listen for Miles in the background. He would predictably be barking and there wasn't much I could do. But on that Friday night in November, I remember the alarming silence that engulfed me as I walked by the apartment windows.

I swiped my key fob at the outdoor entrance and headed down the building's center hallway. There was still only silence. Usually the barking would resonate even louder in the closed hallway, but tonight there was nothing. Not a peep.

I entered the apartment, threw my bag on the chair and my keys on the counter. I would usually hear his paws prancing on the cage bottom through the door that led to the master suite. Still nothing.

That was until I opened the bedroom door and saw Miles run out into the hallway.

"What the..." I didn't even finish my sentence as I took a few steps. "Oh my..."

His crate was completey flattened. I stared at it in disbelief for a second as Miles pounced on me. I couldn't believe that he escaped. *How was this possible? Was Miles' anxiety so bad that he would rattle the heavy-duty cage to the point where it could crumble?* Looking at it quickly, I realized that he had pulled the quilt through the top grate so hard that it dislodged the latches that kept the front door attached to the roof of the crate. Nevertheless, it was like a jail break.

But that was only part of the problem.

I surveyed the damage. If I thought the blinds in the second bedroom were dinged up from the incident two months prior, then this large blind covering three windows was officially decimated as there were big gaps in between the slats from where he appeared to hang on them like monkey bars. The standup mirror was tipped over and shards of glass speckled the carpet. The fluff of the comforter was spread around the room in bits and pieces.

And just as I turned around, Miles was dragging a bottle of bleach from the bathroom across the carpet. His teeth had punctured the outside of the gallon-sized bottle and he was spilling the chemical wherever he dragged it.

"Miles what are you doing?" I shouted, growing more frustrated with the situation. I took the leaking bottle out of his mouth and put it on the shower floor. If I only had that mirror to look at my reflection, I'm sure my face would not have done my emotions justice at that point. I was frustrated beyond belief as I soaked up the bleach with some paper towels.

I picked up the glass from the broken mirror and vacuumed the rug but despite my earlier efforts, the bleach had already tinged the brown carpet near the bathroom a purplish tan. Fortunately for Miles, the color change would be somewhat hidden by the open door, otherwise I would have burst a blood vessel or two screaming as yet another night's incident took a chunk out of my security deposit.

Ruined blinds. Scratched floors. Stained carpet. It had not even been three months, but when I looked at the apartment, it felt like a lot longer than that. There was no doubt about it, but Miles was doing his best to age both the apartment and his father.

CHAPTER 10

Christmas Eve

"At Christmas, the family is not complete
unless the dog is present."
— Anonymous

'Twas the night before Christmas, And all through the house, Not a creature was stirring..." Well actually, one comes to mind.

Sarah was working the overnight shift on Christmas Eve 2013. I followed the same trend by spending my holiday at the veterinary hospital, but only during the daytime hours. As the second lowest on the totem pole, it was all but guaranteed that I was going to be working on Christmas Eve. It was my first holiday working at the hospital, if you exclude the Fourth of July, Labor Day, and Thanksgiving that I had worked earlier in the year. What was I going to do, I asked myself rhetorically, as I walked through the sliding doors into the hospital waiting room. At least I had my four legged friend to keep me company that day; I decided to bring Miles in to work with me.

The December weather for the 24th day of the month was characteristic for the Northeast for that time of year. The upper twenties with a slight breeze brought about a tingling sensation to the exposed skin. Just two days earlier, the temperatures were uncharacteristically in the mid sixties. Go figure. The hope was that the weather would keep the crowds down, especially at the closing hour of four in the afternoon. The only way this would get better is if snow began to fall. Precipitation kills business, I quickly learned.

I placed my bookbag on my desk, punched in, and brought Miles over to his cage. He grew to like his metal confinement, and I began to think it was because he felt safe from the sticks, pokes, and usual veterinary activities that he witnessed through its steel-wired front door. Unlike at home where I needed to bribe him with a peanut butter Kong to go into his crate, he would jump right in to his cage at work as if it was his sanctuary. I wasn't surprised.

"Good morning Doc," the familiar voice of Mike rang in my ears as he squeezed my shoulders walking by. "Ready for a fun day?"

"Merry Christmas," I grunted, glancing at him out of the corner of my eye. Mike, a veterinary assistant at the hospital, was a 20-year-old college student who was still looking for his direction in life. Aren't we all at times?

"So, I see Miles is sporting his holiday present still," he joked, as he motioned with his hands around his neck, referring to my dog's shock collar.

It was just last week when the barking reached its fever pitch. Miles was lying down in his cage, his eyes closed, apparently sleeping on his orange blanket, at least so I thought. The treatment room was quiet. Dr. Scherz and a technician were readying themselves to take blood from a cat's back leg when one shrill "woof" erupted from his cage. I wasn't the only one jumpy at that point. The cat jumped off the table and clawed its way up the wall cages, eventually running loose on the floor of the treatment room. And all I heard were grumbles from the complaint department.

"MILES!" Dr. Scherz screamed, "Come on I was right there," she sighed. Her disgust was evident. I knew that I needed to douse her anger right there. I scolded Miles, but my intentions for doing so were clear. The last thing I needed was for my fellow colleague to complain about Miles being at the workplace. Knowing how mopey and moody Dr. Scherz could become, I didn't want to push my limits or cause any trouble. I knew damn well that I didn't have any options with Miles, and I couldn't afford to fool around. Day-care was off limits because they closed before I left work. It would do me, him, and my wallet no good to keep him there overnight on a regular basis. And forget the thought of leaving him home alone at the apartment. He'd bark for ten hours, people would complain, his cover would be blown, and the idea of 'going dark' and staying in the shadows would be exposed in this under thirty-five pound community. That night I went home and ordered a shock-collar from Amazon.

For the most part, Miles had become used to his cage at the hospital. But when he wanted to go for a walk, or have a treat, or just some straightforward attention, he would bark. And bark some more. That piercing noise would initially begin as a borderline whimper before transitioning to a low rumbling growl en route to an all out chorus of yips and yaps. With that in mind and knowing what happened in the past with Dr. Scherz and the cat, I introduced Miles to his collar. And by that, I mean I used the vibration mode on his collar, not the shock component. The latter I felt was too harsh. Hey, I wanted my dog to respect and like me, not worry when I was going to use the cruel and unusual punishment of a shock collar to zap him. The hospital wasn't going to be turned into Guantanamo prison. From that point on, the sight of me holding the remote control in my hand or even placing it in my pocket was enough to keep him mindful and quiet. That was the case until he heard the rattle of his chain when it was time to go home at night, and then all bets were off. All in all, it was a good investment. For one, it was as if the device paid for itself within the first couple of days by me bringing Miles to work instead of paying a hundred bucks to drop him off at day care. And two, it allowed Miles to be around his dad on days he couldn't stay home by himself.

Working on Christmas Eve, or any holiday, had its ups and downs. As I would tell my dad, the crazies come out on these types of days. A holiday would go something like this. It would start off pretty quiet, and then all hell would break loose. There would almost always be an owner that would walk in with his dog to tell me that Fido has had bloody diarrhea and been vomiting for the past week, knowing all too well that his pooch was here either due to the fact that he was having company for the holiday, the rugs and house were getting soiled, or his wife was screaming. Perhaps a combination of the above and not necessarily ranked in that order. And by the way, when an owner says a day, they mean two. When they say a few days, that translates to almost a week, and when they say a week, oh God, all bets are off; they really mean two or more. I'm pretty convinced that certain people could give two shits about their animals, no pun intended. If the dog is able to scurry outside in the nick of time to have their version of Montezuma's revenge all over the yard for hours or even days, that's okay. But as soon as one drop falls on their imported wood floors or white carpet, some owners' mindsets will change. Yet if the owners themselves were to simply have an isolated episode of diarrhea or even visualize one drop of blood in their own stool, they'd immediately go rummage through their medicine cabinet or be on their way to the hospital, respectively.

My first Christmas Eve in the office went something like this. After getting Miles settled, I looked at the drop-off board to learn that I had two surgeries scheduled. What the hell, it's Christmas Eve people. Don't you have anything better to do? A

120-pound Rottweiler spay and a fractious cat spay. How am I going to do this by 4 pm? Well, that was an omen for the rest of the day. Fortunately, the staff was playing a joke on me and the day was simply appointment based with no surgeries. I laughed, only because the last thing I wanted was to be by myself in the clinic and have my hands in the bloody abdomen of a huge Rottie as I search for an ovary.

For the morning, the normal occasional stream of people came in with their pets, whether it was for an ear infection or vaccines. Not a big deal. Straight forward. Had my lunch in the designated noon hour. Three more hours until Christmas. All was well. That was until the one o'clock hour came about. The expected case of a dog with none other than hemorrhagic gastroenteritis (yeah, doesn't sound good) strolled in, followed by a walk-in for lameness, topped off by a hit-by-car at 3:45 pm. Stabilized that dog, placed an intravenous catheter, collected some blood, took some radiographs. After all was said and done, the Boston Terrier was stable, but I still recommended overnight monitoring for her at the 24-hour veterinary hospital down the road. The time was now 6:00 pm. And with all the commotion, I didn't even hear a peep from Miles as the prospect of missing Christmas Eve Mass entered my mind.

As an Italian who was raised as a Catholic, church and Christmas went together like peanut butter and jelly. I didn't want to miss Christmas Eve mass, for I knew that I had sinned by not going for the past fifty-one weeks of the year. No excuses God. Knowing that I wasn't going to be able to meet up with my parents for mass in their home town prior to dinner, I wrapped up my medical notes and Googled the nearest Catholic Church.

"Come on Miles," I said as I picked up his leash, igniting his stockpile of energy. His tail pounded the sides of the solid steel cage while his paws pranced on the bottom. Attaching the leash was the hard part, as the metal ring on his collar was a moving target. And like every other time, he would jump on me, over and over again. And if he wasn't hopping, he was trying to mouth my wrist.

"Miles, stop. *Miles stop! STOP!*" It could go on for five minutes if we didn't get going. As we went by the pharmacy, his tail knocked over the bottles on the lower shelf. Foil stripped packages of amoxicillin pills were scattered on the floor. Plastic bottles containing carprofen chewables and cefpodoxime caplets rolled around on the ground. "Wait. *WAIT,*" I instructed. I didn't need him munching on these. Bending over to pick up the bottles, I felt his front paws on the back of my neck as he sniffed and nudged his muzzle into my face. The jangle of his metal chain fainted into the background as his whimper of excitement grew louder. The pace of his tail picked up, and he began to hop on his back legs. See what I mean, it's like a cycle, a never-ending cycle.

As the sliding doors at the exit opened, the frozen winter air hit my face with a rude awakening. Miles welcomed the feeling because that was the sensation of freedom, especially after being held captive in his cage for the past ten hours. He dragged me over to the grass on the side of the building for a quick pee, and then we both ran to the car.

My car's engine sputtered and stuttered as I turned the key in the ignition. The cold was taking its toll on more than just my extremities but also my ten-year-old car. I knew all too well that there wasn't going to be heat in the near future as I pulled out of the lot. I raced down Route 22 to St. Mary's Church-Stony Hill, a Catholic church located in town. I still had my ancient Samsung flip phone, so I had to rely on my memory for directions. There was no Google maps app on that phone. It was 6:20 pm when I pulled into the church parking lot. I had ten minutes before the ceremonial procession began, but I watched the sequence of church patrons file through the rustic, stained-glass wood doors at the church entrance from my car. An older couple, probably in their late 70s, walked arm in arm up the stairs to the entryway. The man was wearing a vintage flat cap and navy suit. His wife sported a long, black pea coat. Traditional attire for the holiday. And here I was wearing my light blue, blood-spotted, fur covered scrubs. I chuckled at the contrast, but what left a lasting impression was a trail of their frozen breath as it hit the evening air. A sense of uneasiness filled my insides. I prayed that Miles wouldn't freeze to death. For the next five minutes, I blasted the heat, hoping that there would be some residual warmth remaining when I pulled the key from the ignition. I headed into the church and took my seat in the back left corner. The pews outlined the marble altar in a near semi-circle. The ends of the three aisles and perimeter of the altar were lined with Poinsettia flowers. Classic decorations including white-lighted Christmas trees, pine roping, and candles were located throughout. What could be better than the tranquility of Christmas Eve? As the calmness of the night filled the church, I found myself thinking about the blur of the past year. The end of my schooling career, a new job, and the fresh start of living life entered my mind. I wouldn't be telling the truth if I told you I wasn't counting down the minutes to the end of mass. Little Buddy, as Sarah liked to say, was in the car. And as the last blessing was pronounced, I hustled out to the car, looking from afar if I would be able to see his silhouette through the back window. But the view was obscured by the adhered frost of snowflakes, individually displayed in a random pattern over the car's windows.

"Let's get some heat on bud," I said, as I brought my car's engine back to life. Miles was sitting up, his tail in full motion. Within a few minutes, the heat was pumping, the Christmas tunes were blaring, and we were ready to celebrate Christmas Eve with the family. *Easier said than done.* This would be Mile's first holiday with people other than his parents and 'grandparents.' The more people there were, the rowdier he tended to become. Knowing that, I crossed my fingers as I pulled into my parents' driveway.

Ding dong. I rang the door bell as I characteristically did at my parents. My dad loved seeing Miles greet him on the front steps, so I kept this routine going.

"There he is!" my dad exclaimed, laughing as Miles was going berserk on the porch. Nothing new there. "Oh, hi Phil," he belatedly remarked as he gave me his characteristic hug. Miles was chomping at the bit to go explore the new smells and sights. Knowing there was going to be ham, lasagna, new guests, and new friends, I chose to keep the leash attached. It was my hopeful attempt to try and keep control of this carnivorous creature, at least for the time being.

As we walked in, the beast plowed down the hallway and led me straight into the kitchen where the full smorgasbord was on display. My brother had just taken the ham out of the oven, and placed it next to the lasagna on the kitchen island. All kinds of cookies were lined on the counter in their trademark metal Christmas tins. Snowball, chocolate crinkles, hello dollies. There were enough cookies for five families. Miles ran right over to the vicinity to get as close as he could before I gave him a tug on the leash. The Johnsons, who were longtime family friends of my parents dating back to my elementary school years, were sitting in the living room. Fortunately, they loved animals and have had dogs of their own in the past. They knew what it would be like, or so I hoped.

We conversed for a bit as the lasagna, hot out of the oven, had the chance to rest. For my Italian father, it was almost a sin if we didn't give the lasagna the chance to set before serving it. That gave us a few minutes to catch up with each other. I gave Miles his dinner to keep him entertained until we sat down ourselves. It was nearly 8 o'clock, well past his usual 7 o'clock dinner time. As he chomped away, Mrs. Johnson asked about my new addition, and Mr. Johnson chirped in with questions about my job. He had recently retired from working nearly forty years for the railroad company, and he encouraged me by reminding me that I only had about thirty more to go.

The easiest part of the night was over as my dad announced dinner time. We sat around the dining room table, decorated in the traditional green cloth. And then there was Miles. There he was, sitting next to my chair as he waited with hope that a morsel would fall from my plate in the upcoming moments.

"...Thank you God for a bountiful blessing," my dad concluded grace. So far so good. Food wasn't being eaten yet, so that's probably why things were going well. I could tell out of the corner of my eye that Miles head was going back and forth. Once he figured out who the vulnerable table member was and what was where on the table, he was going to be drawn to that person or spot like a shark to blood. I made certain not to make eye contact with him, for that would be like giving him an invitation to the party. I was hoping he would hang in there, perhaps lay down, or simply take a nap. I took two bites.

And then it began.

First the low-pitched growling started to rumble from within, which I tried to ignore as I continued eating. I was hoping that the repetitive movement of the fork from the plate to my mouth would distract him with the false hope that a piece of pasta would fall off. It didn't. He began to prod his nose under my elbow to try and get a better look at what he wanted to eat so very much. I resisted his urge, but that only caused him to look for another opportunity with someone else. He circled the table, finding the same response with my parents, en route to my brother, who pushed his face away.

"Woof!" Miles barked once, its pitch causing me to jolt in my seat and redirect my eyes in his direction. Mrs. Johnson was to my left, and I recall her leaning over, giving me a nudge, and with a smile saying, "He's got quite the bark." I'm sure my tension was palpable at that time. But like she has always done, Mrs. Johnson put everything in perspective and kept things light, almost preparing me for the slippery slope that we were going to be going down. She had been there before with her dogs.

"*WOOF, WOOF!*" The barking grew louder and repetitive. He now had my undivided attention.

As I got up from the table, Miles scurried away in the opposite direction, but couldn't escape my pursuit as I grasped his collar. "No! NO! *Sit*," I instructed. He obeyed for the moment. As my mom praised him in the background for being a good listener, I knew his good behavior would only be temporary. I was shaking my head, not because I was surprised, but because I knew he was only going to get worse. I took my seat again at the table. Within thirty seconds of being reprimanded, he was at it again, circling and sniffing each place setting.

"No Miles," my mom paused before looking at him closer. "Oh no, Phil," she paused. "He's chewing the table cloth. Stop! Stop!" she pleaded.

I couldn't see him on the other side of the table. The vision of him tearing at the cloth, latching onto it with his teeth, and pulling away as I approached entered my mind. I didn't want to imagine the China dishware and glassware flying off the table. Just like that, Christmas Eve could turn into a disaster. I snapped out of it, leaving those thoughts behind.

"You want a treat?" I asked in desperation, knowing that the dinner option was already exhausted. And just like that, he was at my side. The tablecloth was suddenly old news and the threat on Christmas Eve ended. *Works every time*, I snickered.

Having a backup plan for the evening was a part of my planning. I went to his travel bag on the kitchen table and took out his peanut butter-stuffed bone. The only problem was that there wasn't much peanut butter remaining. A new one of these would leave little worry, as he would suck, lick, slurp, chew, crunch, and drool over it for hours. The fact that this one was an old and skimpy-filled bone would come back to haunt me, I realized. Within five minutes, he was at it again, this time barking non-stop. Unbelievable. *Didn't we just address this*, I asked myself rhetorically. By then, I was beyond frustrated, as I sprung out of my chair yet again. With one eye on his bone and one eye on me, Miles backpedaled into the kitchen. And though he retreated, he kept his tail wagging. It was like a relentless back and forth game that I would never win.

As I was about to sit down, it dawned on me. Where was Miles? Something wasn't right. For an attention-seeking dog plagued by separation anxiety, it was uncharacteristic for Miles to stay by himself in another room in the house, especially on Christmas Eve. When I went to go check on him in the kitchen, I turned the corner to the sight of two white paws on the center island. His neck was extended as far as possible as he was putting all of his effort into nibbling the top of the baked ham.

"*MILES, get down,*" I whispered directly into his ear, being careful not to draw my mother's attention. I pulled him down, knowing damn well if my mom found out that her Christmas ham was being lapped up by Miles, I may very well be in the dog house myself.

My dad asked from the other room if there was a problem, but I reassured him and my mom that everything was fine.

"I'm going to go put Miles in the car," I shouted across the room. I just didn't tell them which car.

It was too cold to put Miles outside. Yeah, I did have him outside about an hour ago when I was at church, but I thought that the garage would be a much more pleasant option. First off, it was warmer in there since he would be sheltered from the colder winter elements. Secondly, if he started to bark, it wouldn't draw as much attention, especially if the neighbors and carolers were outside at some point. *Don't need to have a police report under the tree tomorrow,* I chortled, as I shut the door to my dad's Hyundai Sonata.

But the usual tranquility of Christmas Eve was not meant to be, as the serenity brought on by the back seat of both Sarah's Subaru and my Hyundai did not carry over to my father's vehicle for our furry friend. As I sat down and continued to share in the feast, my attention veered off to the faint whining in the background. The women were talking about the winter television schedule including the upcoming season of American Idol. The men were voicing their frustrations with corporate bullshit and the future of retirement. And for me, well, I just sat there listening. The radio station New Jersey

101.5 was playing their thirty-six straight hours of commercial free Christmas music. At that moment, all I could think about was Andy Williams singing his version of "Silent Night." How ironic, heh. Classic tunes couldn't even drown out Miles.

Once the dining room table was cleared and the area was deemed to be as dog-proof as possible for a holiday get-together, I brought Miles back into the house. I couldn't leave him in the cage all day and the car all night, could I?

But maybe I should have.

His excitement was not dampened one bit by his time in isolation as he exploded through the entryway connecting the garage with the kitchen. It was his way of saying, 'I'm baaack!!' In fact, he worked himself up so much that he went straight for the water bowl and lapped up every drop. The bowl was dry within a minute. Not a drop left. Grandpa came by and filled it up with some crushed ice, which Miles always confused for cold, liquid chew treats.

"He must be getting tired," my mom noted, as she arranged the cookies on different platters. Was she talking to me?

For the rest of the night, I reversed our roles and pretended that I was his shadow. I tended to notice on days like that, when there were new people, smells, and temptations, that nothing good could happen after 9 o'clock at night. *It was kind of like children on overdrive*, I imagined.

As I drank my coffee and scarfed down chocolate crinkles at the kitchen island, I kept one eye on my dog and one eye on the cookie platter. I always had this informal, fraternal challenge with my brother as to who could eat more cookies. As the competition continued into the final stretch, I peered around the corner to see what was left on the serving dish.

Three snowballs. Two crinkles. Four cannolis. One cream puff. Oh wait, was I looking at my mother's dessert plate? (Just kidding, I love you Mom!)

Dessert was a word that everyone in the Casale household would attentively listen for. Thinking back, the only time my parents in the past twenty plus years didn't have a cup of coffee and some type of cake or sweet at night was when my dad was away on business. Having said that, my dad hadn't eaten a cookie in twenty years, and he would much rather indulge in something healthier. It's funny. Actually, it's ridiculous. To this day, my dad has this belief that having apple pie is healthier because it contains fruit, but whenever I bring up to him that one and a half cups of sugar are poured over the apples in that preservative-filled, artificially flavored store bought crust, he seems to act like that doesn't count. "It has apples and spices," he would say, as he would often go into a culinary diatribe on how his semi-homemade pie is healthier than other desserts.

Like 'dadda' or 'mamma' for a baby, the words 'treat' and 'dessert' resonated with Miles as well and were two of the first vocabulary words that he learned in our apartment. It was a must, not just because we wanted to have our dog trained, but for when we needed him to behave. There's a big difference between having your dog sit upon command while on a walk outside versus following that same instruction on a Christmas Eve when he's out of control. To say the least, this holiday was the perfect example. When the time-out session and multiple verbal corrections failed to calm the beast, it was that famous bone-shaped Milkbone treat that did the trick. When I broke this cookie into pieces, the sight and smell of his favorite treat not only brought Miles' wild side to an immediate halt, but unveiled the observant focus characteristic for his breed.

Wow. I was always amazed at the power of some processed wheat flour and bone meal.

This allowed me to have a somewhat relaxing dessert time, for his concentration was not on the dining room table, the guests, or any other distraction, but instead on the broken pieces of those scrumptious treats lined up on the kitchen island. *When's he going to give me one,* I'm sure he pondered as the drool came out of his mouth. That continued until the Johnson family left.

I texted Sarah, "Tonight, I worked overtime. Hope Santa brings you something good."

I plopped down on the family room couch. It was the first minute I sat down all day. The lights of the Christmas tree were reflecting off of the darkened television screen. The flames inside of the fireplace flickered, their light bouncing off of the glass and porcelain ornaments. Red stockings dangled from the mantle. Our names, written in gold glitter, glimmered in the continual dance of the orange flames. Miles was curled up in a tiny ball underneath his stocking, enjoying the warmth of the fire. Then it dawned on me. Perhaps this was his first Christmas Eve, ever. That's what I wanted to believe, I decided, as I continued to write his biography in my mind. I glanced at the pile of children books from my youth that my mom had annually arranged in front of the hearth, noting that my favorite, *The Night Before Christmas*, was on top of the stack. *How appropriate,* I smiled, as I looked back at Miles and watched his eyes begin to fade, knowing all too well, we 'had just settled our brains for a long winter's nap.'

CHAPTER 11

Car Search

"Dogs love to go for rides. A dog will happily get into any vehicle going anywhere." — Dave Barry, Austrian zoologist

I knew when I started searching for my new car that I wanted an SUV that could carry my golf clubs and my dog. And that's all I knew.

My 2002 Hyundai Accent was my first car. I purchased it for about $10,000 after working and saving my money from the time that I was fourteen years of age. This four-cylinder, fuel economical vehicle took me from place A to B for more than a decade. From driving down the road to the grocery store to making the cross country trek to Oklahoma multiple times, my ride was reliable but getting old.

After eleven years, normal wear and tear had started to take its toll on my car and my wallet. Fortunately, there were no major problems involving the transmission or engine, but smaller problems like worn down, squeaky brakes were starting to pile up. Though fixable, every small problem had labor charges associated with it, and that's when I decided that I didn't want to put money into a decade old car. Let the new car search begin!

For anyone that knows me, I'm as meticulous of an individual as one could imagine. I like to know every detail, every who, what, when, where, why, and how of every situation that I become invested in. *Why shouldn't that be the case*, I always ask myself. From work to recreational activities, I have always thought things through every way possible. When it comes to my job, I always think outside of the box. What am I missing? I want to know more than is needed, just in case something new comes up. I replay scenarios over and over in my mind to ensure that all areas are covered. Look, when I'm motivated and interested in something, no one will surpass my drive as I accomplish my goal. I will have everything covered inside and out. With that mindset, I began my search for my new ride.

I went to Ford, Chevy, Subaru, Honda, Hyundai, and Toyota dealers over and over, just to name a few. I was online every night checking out the Ford Escape, the Honda CRV, learning about the packages for the Chevy Equinox, the prices for the Toyota Rav 4 and Hyundai Tuscon. Essentially when I went to the dealership, I already knew about the car. At that point, I simply wanted to see what it looked like, feel how it drove, and get a quote. I didn't need a dealer to sell me a car. In my mind, they were just the middle men who could only persuade me with a dollar sign. If I was going to be spending tens of thousands of dollars on a car, I'd better put the extra effort in before I signed on the dotted line.

I hadn't been shopping for a car in a long time, and I was amazed at the bells and whistles. This feature, that feature, this package, that option. It can become expensive. I remember building my dream car, the Jeep Grand Cherokee, online. V6 engine. Four wheel drive. Leather seats. Chrome finishes. All weather package. When I saw the price tag of $44,000, I laughed out loud unexpectedly. It wasn't soon after that I decided, 'No, I don't need heated rear passenger seats or the chrome package for an additional premium price.' What I did need was enough room in the cargo area for Miles because there was zero chance of him riding in the back seat like he had done for the past eight months in my old car.

Both Sarah and I saw the effects that Miles had on the back seat of her new Subaru. Fur embedded in the car seats. Nail punctures on the leather center console. Muddy paw prints on the black interior. I did not want my new car to have any of that.

So for the first three weeks that I had my new Hyundai Santa Fe, there was one rule: no dogs allowed. If we had to go somewhere, we'd take Sarah's car. Let her car be the sacrificial lamb, not mine. Until the WeatherTech cargo and floor liners were delivered, I was going to preserve that freshness and new car smell for as long as possible.

I also purchased the WeatherTech pet barrier with the goal of keeping Miles in the cargo area. That's where I pick up our story, with the first day Miles traveled in our new SUV, and what I thought might have been his last.

We were heading down the back roads behind our apartment on our way to the park on a Sunday morning in early April 2014. We were probably on the road for about two minutes when our son's separation anxiety reminded me why I purchased the barrier in the first place. Because he was unable to roam free in the apartment without tearing up pillows or pulling down curtains, he either needed to go in his crate or ride in the car when we left the apartment. And on days like this April morning when he came for a ride with us, the only way to keep him from damaging the car seats or putting indents in the interior was to keep him in the cargo area. I laid the second row of seats down, giving him a straight on view of his mother and father in the hope that an unobstructed view would calm his fears. Well, it didn't. As I alluded to earlier, his anxiety was tangible, and began with a whimper, then exploded into a series of startling, repetitive yelps. And just like that, in my rear view mirror, I watched him crawl under the lowest bar of the barrier and across the second row of passenger seats. Within seconds, his paw was attached to my right shoulder. I jammed on the brakes and pulled into an empty parking lot of an antique shop. I was in full disbelief.

"How is this possible," I screamed, growing more infuriated as each second passed. My blood pressure was off the charts. I stormed out of the car shouting, "Why can't you just be like every other dog?"

Sarah gave me that 'why did you say that' glare as she opened up the side door, allowing Miles to jump down to freedom. Mumbling to myself, I raised the second row seats and started checking them for any pulls or punctures. I dusted the fur off onto the floor.

"Up," I instructed Miles, as I opened up the cargo door. He jumped thirty inches from the ground into the back of the SUV with ease and no coaxing. I realized getting him into the cargo area was much easier than his crate at home. Keeping him in there may be the difficult part.

"Let's hope he stays in there this time," Sarah joked as she poked me in my side. Little did we know that within two minutes we were going to be in the same situation.

"What the...,"I jammed on the brakes and pulled off the road into the shoulder. It was like it was in slow motion as I remained helpless watching Miles climb *over* the top grate of the pet barrier. By now I felt my rage pulsing through my body, evident by my temporal vein bulging as reflected in the rearview mirror.

I started screaming about Miles, the cost of my car, the importance of keeping it clean, the reason I purchased the WeatherTech products, and so on. I knew all too well that I simply needed to raise the last bar on the pet barrier to the ceiling to prevent him from jumping. I gave him a few inches, and he took advantage. Recognizing the situation, Sarah let me vent as she walked Miles around outside in the adjacent woods. I disassembled the barrier and put it in the backseat.

For the rest of our morning ride to and from the park, I drove alone in the front seat. Why? Because Miles and his mother were sitting together in the cargo area.

You know what, all I could do was smile as I looked at the two of them in the back. I didn't want to soften my tough stance on his behavior, but it wasn't easy as I tried to wipe that smirk off my face before Sarah would see it.

This dog was smart, and he reminded me of that yet again on that Sunday morning.

CHAPTER 12

Football Sundays

*"The NFL owns a day of the week. The
same day the Church used to own.
Now it's theirs."*
— Dr. Cyril Wecht, played by Albert Brooks,
in the 2015 movie *Concussion*

Growing up from the time that I was five years old, I relied on the National Football League to help me get through the week. As a Giants fan since kindergarten, I grew up watching a New York team that, for the most part, just wasn't that good in the 1990s, outside of the 1990 championship team that I was too young to remember. From missing the playoffs for five out of six seasons in the early part of the decade to that heartbreaking 23-22 loss to the Minnesota Vikings in the 1998 Wild Card playoff game, I clearly wasn't watching football as a front-runner. My team always seemed to fall short of the San Francisco 49ers and could never escape the shadow of America's team, the Dallas Cowboys, who combined to win four championships in the first five years of the 1990s decade.

Over the years, I have watched football for different reasons. In my elementary school years I watched the Giants because I wanted to brag to my friends, particularly a classmate named Anthony who was a Cowboys' fan. For three of the first four years that we went to school together, his team won the Super Bowl while mine would miss the playoffs. After two consecutive losing seasons, I remember the Monday morning in November of 1993 when I came into my third-grade classroom, floating on cloud nine after the afternoon game the day before. A Sunday afternoon, game winning 54-yard field goal by Giants' kicker Brad Daluiso paired with a Cowboys loss a few days earlier on Thanksgiving made that a memorable morning in the classroom, one that I still think of to this day. On a side note, the Cowboys went on to win the Super Bowl yet again that season.

When my parents moved in 1995, my transition to a different middle school was not easy for me, especially since it took place in the middle of a 5th grade academic year. Having no friends and being bullied on a daily basis was a difficult combo for me, one that you never want to know what is like. During that time football Sundays was my salvation. I loved waking up and watching the funny, lighthearted FOX pregame show with James Brown, Terry Bradshaw and crew, knowing that I had a slew of games ahead of me to watch. The voices of ESPN's Chris Berman and Tom Jackson, the hosts of the popular evening football recap show *NFL PRIMETIME*, helped soothe my Sunday night blues. When their show ended at 8:30, it was almost as if the anxiety of Monday morning had come early.

In the years that followed, especially during my veterinary school years, I relied on football as much for entertainment as I did for an escape. Throughout my ten years of hitting the books, taking tests, and feeling the increased stress of the academic profession, I leaned on Sunday football to keep me sane. It helped me clear my mind. From the pregame show at noon to the final whistle of the Sunday night primetime telecast twelve hours later, I enjoyed every minute, so much so that when I was out in Oklahoma, I would switch my Sunday emergency veterinary shift for *two* midweek shifts, just so I wouldn't miss a game. It wasn't about football as much as it was about my sanity.

As you can tell, football Sundays were and remain an important part of my life. I have always felt that sports are the greatest diversion from reality while remaining the greatest form of reality television. Forget about *American Idol, Dancing with the Stars,* or *The Bachelor.* For me, watching football on Sunday has been as American as apple pie.

By now, it should come as no shock to you that my to-do list on Sundays between the months of September and February has always included watching football. Well, it just so happens that Sarah has a tendency to always plan my Sundays in the fall. From apple-picking to walking the pumpkin patches to Christmas tree hunts, we always conveniently had something to do on football Sunday. Great. Just great. And thanks to Miles, Sarah added another activity to my weekend agenda come September 2014.

"Guess what, I spoke with the trainer Kathy from the other day," she began. "I enrolled Miles in a training course."

I was watching a game so I was listening in and out, but when Sarah remarked, "there's just one thing," I picked up the remote and muted the broadcast.

"It's on Sunday afternoons, so you're going to need to bring Miles. It's only eight sessions," Sarah noted optimistically, pointing out that she would bring him if her work schedule allowed.

Two months! During football season! And during afternoon games! I couldn't believe it. I asked if there were morning sessions or if we could change to Thursdays, the other day I was off work during the week. No luck there, as this was the only time that her training course was offered.

It was just one week later when I packed up a bag of kibble and drove Miles to the town of Hillsborough for his first training session. I had to be there for a 3 o'clock session so I left about a half hour early to ensure that I would get there on time. Fortunately I had my radio set to 660 AM, the FAN, to hear the broadcast up until the midway part of the third quarter.

I remember arriving early and debating with myself if this was going to be worthwhile. I heard Miles whimpering in the back seat and pacing back and forth as we saw different dogs walking around outside. Though I questioned the value of yet another training session, I knew all too well that if I were at home, Miles would be jumping and barking as soon as I tried to sit on the couch. The fact was that Miles needed the training, as I was reminded earlier in the afternoon that the only way to watch a game in quiet with him was to stand for three hours.

The training session was held in the empty parking lot of a veterinary hospital. There were eight dogs including a beautiful Irish Setter and a couple of feisty terriers. I was gripping onto Miles leash tightly, but just like the time I saw him in the PETSMART adoption event, he remained calm and unbothered by the surrounding dogs. The trainer Kathy introduced herself to me and asked me to describe some of my concerns with Miles.

"How much time do you have," I asked facetiously. In a way, I wasn't kidding. I listed a couple of his problems, which she wrote down on her notepad. She went down the line and within a few minutes of introducing herself to the class, we began our session. Her focus at first was on working on the basic commands like sit, stay, and come. Sounds simple, right? Guess again. It was a chaotic scene at first. This small, black and white terrier next to Miles was bouncing around the parking lot and the owner couldn't keep him in his assigned training block. He kept barking at any dog that approached his spot. Other dogs weren't much better. The Irish Setter, though he had an amazing coat, seemed to have left his brain in the car. His owner was talking about showing his purebred at different competitions, but all I could think about was how this jittery dog couldn't stay still for two seconds, let alone follow a basic command. And the tan Shih Tzu did nothing but lay down on the pavement, her motivation non-existent as her aloof demeanor resisted her owner's demands. I wasn't all that surprised, as my mind transitioned back to the late middle school years when I walked my neighbor's stubborn dog, Harley.

All the while, the best dog in the class was none other than... Miles. I couldn't believe it! His keen focus put the other dogs' efforts to shame and did justice to the narrative of the Border Collie breed's intelligence. His ability to comprehend commands paired with his precision and rapidity in executing those orders was great to see because it showed me that he could do these things, that is when he wanted to. Now of course I don't think that I would have had as much success with our first session if I didn't have the bag of kibble. Without that enticement, who knows what would have transpired for that forty-five minute session. Thank you Purina.

In the final few minutes of our class, Kathy recapped what we had gone over in the afternoon session. Oh, and she gave us homework. I remember muttering, 'Is she serious?' After twenty-three years of school, I didn't want to have one more assignment at home. Training sessions were essentially about training the owner and relying on the informed owner to execute the new orders at home. I placed the folded paper into my fleece jacket pocket and hustled off to the car.

I put on the radio again and heard Bob Pappa's postgame report. Phew. Giants 30, Texans 17. Seven more sessions to go. I could only hope that one of those weeks included a Giant's bye.

When we arrived home, Sarah had just woken up and was getting her lunch ready for work. I burst through the apartment door and shouted, "He's the best student in the class!" With that, Miles raced into the kitchen and began jumping on Sarah uncontrollably.

"Is that true Miles," she questioned as she dodged Miles latest bound. "I just might think that your daddy's not telling me the truth."

CHAPTER 13

Sick As A Dog

*"Such short little lives our pets have to spend
with us, and they spend most of it waiting
for us to come home each day."*
— John Grogan, American novelist

January 2014.

"He's peeing everywhere," Sarah confided over the phone,
looking for my medical advice, as she followed Miles around
his grandma's house with a towel. This 10 o'clock evening
consultation was free, but I wish it wasn't as I rubbed my eyes
after falling asleep on the couch.

From what Sarah told me, Miles wouldn't stop peeing inside
her mother's home. She took him up to Connecticut for a long
weekend, but he didn't start to show this uncharacteristic
behavior until later in the day. He'd dribble urine in the living
room, so she'd take him outside. Twenty minutes later he was
whining at the front door to go outside. Thirty minutes after
that, he would have the urge to urinate again, but would let
loose on the wood floors. I wasn't embarrassed with Miles'
actions because I knew it wasn't behavioral, but because he
was sick.

Sarah took him to a veterinarian that I recommended in
Hartford, Connecticut in the morning. Urinary tract infection.
Ten days of cefpodoxime. For Miles the best part of taking an
antibiotic was that it needed to be given with food.

I'm sure holding in his urine while sitting in a cage at my work for ten plus hours straight the past two days didn't help him much. In fact, I'm sure that contributed to his ailment.

I have always been amazed how Miles could lick the ground, ingest deer feces, chew on a squirrel carcass, lap up stagnant water, or do what dogs do on an everyday basis without ever getting sick. If you saw where his Kong chew toy went, you could see where my worries stem from. Knock on wood, but if I did what he did, I would be in the hospital. This is coming from the guy who thinks about getting a winter cold and ends up bed-ridden with the flu two days later.

In all my time of working around animals, either as a veterinary student at Oklahoma State or in practice in New Jersey, I have seen a lot of ill dogs. Thinking back at some of the sickest dogs that I've seen, I recall those dogs suffering from parvovirus, a life-threatening gastrointestinal virus that is often accompanied by excessive vomiting and diarrhea. They were in the ICU at the OSU teaching hospital and were essentially flooded with continuous intravenous fluids, antibiotics, along with anti-vomiting and anti-nausea drugs for days, if not weeks. Over the years, I've seen dogs suffer from different illnesses including hemorrhagic gastroenteritis, Giardiasis, and Salmonellosis. Take my word when I say that these intestinal conditions are not pretty.

With that in the back of my mind, I had made it my top priority to make sure that our dog was put in the best position to succeed and stay healthy. I have always been the worried parent around Miles. If you were to spend a couple days with me, you would undoubtedly hear me say, "Don't go there, come back, watch out, don't eat that, leave it, careful," to name a few of my common sayings.

And despite my good intentions and watchful eye, I learned sometimes you can only do so much.

That brings us to the night of Saturday, June 7, 2014. I came home from work to the sound of silence. Now, contrary to my thoughts eight months earlier, I was happy that Miles was quiet in his crate. It didn't cross my mind that perhaps he was up to no good. In the past, I would be worried if I didn't hear him yelping through the door. What's wrong, what's he up to, what trouble am I going to stumble across? But in recent months, I was relieved to hear the hum of the air conditioner or chirp of the birds instead when I stepped out of my vehicle. He had grown accustomed to Sarah's evening work routine and his crate. It was the new norm.

Well on that Saturday night, the only thing different when I opened the master bedroom door was the pungent smell. I wasn't sure what it was at first. Turning on the light, I saw Miles lying down in his crate, his black coat splattered with brown specks.

I was worried, but when I squatted down to unlock the cage, my concern evolved into an all out panic. The perimeter of his crate was surrounded by a solid two inches of diarrhea.

The crate looked and smelled like a sewer. As did Miles.

"Miles what happened?" I exclaimed, my eyes were wide open as I brainstormed my next step forward, literally.

I didn't know where to start. His white paws were legitimately stained brown as if he jumped ankle deep into a pile of mud. He was covered in feces from head to toe. His muzzle was mottled brown, perhaps from trying to lick himself clean. I guess he had tried to hide the evidence. As soon as I unhitched the locks on the door, he burst out and raced down the wood floors of the hallway to the front door where he started to whimper. That was not like him. In fact, in the nearly twelve months that we had him, he never once raced to the door when I came home from work.

I was in full pursuit, dodging his paw-shaped poop-prints on the way as I surveyed the end table for his leash from afar. 'Where is it, where is it?" I asked myself as I became flustered. When I finally found it and clipped it to his collar, Miles pulled me around the corner and down the three steps leading to the outdoors so fast that by the time my feet were in the grass, he was having explosive diarrhea. Brown-tinged water covered the green grass. Looking back, I didn't care if the neighbors saw him. In fact, I didn't even think about it at that time.

I led Miles back to the apartment door, but picked him up and carried him into the second bathroom where I put him into the shower and closed the sliding doors. I couldn't have him running around the apartment leaving stains everywhere. It would only make the night longer. I tried calling Sarah at her job, but I couldn't reach her. Even when I tried calling the hospital operator, they said that no one with her name worked there. Ay ay ay. *How was that possible*, I asked myself as I regained my focus at the issue at hand.

I proceeded to give Miles a bath, twice. The poop was caked on his paws and the water continued to turn a murky tan as I rubbed his coat.

His diarrhea was so bad that I couldn't even finish drying him off when he raced out of the bathroom to the front door. Here we go again. He stared at the door, then back at me to see if I was coming. I could see the urgency in his eyes as we raced outside. For the next two hours, we would repeat this pattern every five to ten minutes. Oh, and throw in the fact that he vomited up his kibble two separate times.

I had to call my dad. "How's the good doctor doing," my dad characteristically answered the phone. Not good, as I explained the situation. Within twenty minutes, my dad was there helping me clean up. I couldn't do it by myself. Every time I cleaned up one spot in this corner, he would be heaving over in that corner or at the door ready to go out. If I didn't have any help, it would have been worse.

Things quieted down a little after 10 pm. Mercifully, there was nothing left for Miles to get rid of. As he laid down on the couch, I had time to survey the damage. The carpets needed to be shampooed and the shower had to be cleaned. We wrapped up his crate in black garbage bags so that my dad could bring it home to clean with bleach. He told me the next day that he used the pressure washer on it, proving yet again that he would find any reason to take out his new 3000 PSI, gas powered toy. No wonder my dad volunteered to take it home.

The rest of the night I slept on the couch with Miles. I didn't feed him anything before going to bed. As I stretched out, I tried to think back over the past couple of days. What did he eat? Did he get into something? Was he around other dogs? Nothing obvious jumped out at me as I dozed off.

I woke up around six in the morning and looked at the end of the sofa. He was still there, staring at me. *Well, that's good. At least he slept,* I thought. Miles hadn't moved an inch as I'm sure he was drained from the night before. We went for a quick walk outside where he had some loose stool. How was that still possible? Where was it coming from?

Around 9:30 in the morning, we hopped in my car and headed down Route 22 to go to the veterinary hospital I worked at. This was yet another day where I was happy to have that WeatherTech cargo liner in the back, just in case Miles needed to have an accident while I was driving 70 mph down the highway. After an hour at the hospital, all tests came back negative and we left with a couple of medications to help with his diarrhea.

As we walked out through the sliding doors, I looked at Miles as the alpha dog plunged forward, leading the way. His head was held high and his tail wagged side to side. The sun reflected off of his shiny black coat as he pranced along the sidewalk. What a difference twelve hours makes. After a night like that, I think it was fair to say that we both deserved a nap later that afternoon.

CHAPTER 14

CAPE MAY

"In matters of healing the body or the mind, vacation is a true genius!"
— Mehmet Murat ildan, contemporary Turkish novelist

I would be nodding off in one of my pointless general education courses when my flip phone would vibrate, alerting me to a new text message. In it would be a picture of either a sunny, white sand beach with the waves crashing in the background or dinner at the famous Lobster House restaurant.

In the years that I was in college at the University of Connecticut, my parents would always travel down to Cape May for summer vacation. They would always make that trip to the southernmost peninsula in New Jersey after Labor Day. Hotel rates were cut in half. Kids were back in school. No crowds, no long lines, and all the seafood they could imagine. It definitely seemed like a no brainer to go away then compared with the middle of July. At those moments, I wished that I would be playing in the sand or boogey boarding in the ocean rather than sitting in a classroom taking notes on the socioeconomic impact of globalization in India.

Being in college and graduate school for ten years was not easy, but for reasons that you may not be thinking. Sure, going to class sucked. Taking tests sucked even more. Doing that over and over was even worse. But what bothers me the most to this day is the amount of time I spent studying as the precious clock of life continued to tick away. When I graduated in May 2013, my list of things that I wanted to do was so vast that I figured I needed to play a lot of catch up in the game of life. From family time to trips, I wanted to see and do it all. I have never lost that desire or mentality.

Ever.

With that always in mind, Sarah and I began to plan our trip to Cape May in early August 2014. Yes, we were going after Labor Day. And yes, Miles was in the plans to come with us.

I had read somewhere that it is important for your pet to go on vacation. It's good for them to have a change of scenery, the author argued. The article compared the importance and value that a vacation can have on people with the impact it can have on dogs.

"Take a look at this," Sarah said aloud, rotating her Apple laptop. "It's a cottage in Cape May that we can rent. Plus, it's pet friendly."

And with that, Miles was assured that he would be joining us on our long weekend trip. For the past week, and all during our three-and-a-half-hour drive to Cape May, I reiterated to Sarah the wonderful time that my parents had when they went away on vacation. The sun-filled skies, the hot white sand on their toes, and the feel of summer on their skin.

September 8, 2014. Day one of vacation. And my 29th birthday.

Well, when we pulled up to our one bedroom cottage in the early afternoon, the sun was obscured by the gray clouds, and the windshield wipers were whisking away a light drizzle. Go figure. Not much you can do about that as I stepped out of the car.

A thin, white haired woman in her early 60s came down from the back porch and welcomed us. Her name was Joanne, and she lived in the house next door while renting out the cottage to guests during the summer months. She took us on a quick tour of the property and concluded by saying if we needed anything to let her know.

The whole time Miles was going nuts in the backseat of the Subaru. Are you surprised? New place. New person. New everything. Joking with Sarah, I imitated our crazy dog by whispering to her, "Hey dad, where are we now, where are now?' in a goofy voice.

When I let Miles out, he started pulling me as if he were a husky pulling a sled in the Iditarod. His paws left grooves in the rain soaked ground as he clawed his way through the patchy grass onto the screened-in porch. *I guess he didn't want to stand in the rain,* I shrugged.

"Look at the chalkboard," Sarah noted with a smile, pointing at the wall next to the front door.

In light blue chalk, the words 'Cape May Welcomes Sarah and Phil" were written on the board in a teacher-approved, cursive penmanship.

"And Miles," I chirped in as Sarah then wrote his name underneath ours.

We cleaned off Miles' paws before letting him explore the inside of the house. As Miles moseyed from room to room under the watchful eye of his mother, I brought in our suitcases and the ever important crate. We weren't going anywhere without that important piece of metal.

For me, my first night out on the town has always been my favorite evening on vacation. The novelty of exploring the area, learning where the restaurants are and seeing the sights for the first time never wore off.

The only difference on our first night in Cape May was that instead of walking outside, we were driving around in our car as the rain continued to fall.

It was my birthday, may I remind you, so when we walked into the Beachside Bar & Grill, I was happy to see there were televisions. Three words: Monday Night Football.

The Giants were playing the Lions in Detroit, but within the first few minutes of the game, a 67-yard touchdown catch by Detroit's wide receiver Calvin Johnson set the tone for the game, soured my appetite and ominously marked the beginning of the end of yet another poor season for my New York team. I gave Sarah that characteristic look of disgust as the replay showed the two Giants defenders run into each other as if it were Pee Wee football, the collision causing Johnson to become wide open. And when I say 'wide open,' I mean no one else was in the picture on the television except for him.

"What do they do in practice all week," I rhetorically asked. "Same old Giants," as Sarah pushed her Margarita across the table in my direction.

All was forgotten when my blackened Mahi Mahi and fried plantains came out from the kitchen, but only temporarily. That's because the game remained on the big screen just over Sarah's shoulder, so it was tough to avoid.

The restaurant had all of its perimeter windows and doors open to the street so I could easily hear the rain increase in intensity as it bounced off the tops of the cars. After dinner, we rushed outside to our car so we could rescue Miles and head on back to the cottage. Day one of our vacation was a washout.

By next morning, the rain had stopped and the sun was peaking out over the horizon as I stepped onto the porch. The rays, shining from the east, brightened up the wood enclosed deck. I took note of the large seashells that lined the perimeter railings and the decorative sailboats mounted on the walls. Can you tell that I had some time to kill as I waited outside for Sarah to get ready? I wasn't surprised to hear Miles burst open the screen door in pursuit of his father, as the sound of my flip flops clopping on the wood probably drew his attention. He was happier than ever. His excitement and intrigue brought about by his new surroundings were bursting at the seams. He raced back and forth from one door to the next, making sure to avoid the red Adirondack deck chairs lined in his pathway. His occasional whine was his way of vocalizing his eagerness to head out on our morning expedition.

Before long Sarah strolled outside, and we were off. Not knowing where we were going, Miles still wanted to be the leader as he tugged forward on the leash. Following our alpha dog, we headed down a sand covered trail that Joanne had mentioned to us yesterday upon our arrival. It was across the street from our cottage, no wider than two people standing shoulder to shoulder, and no more than a couple hundred yards in length. The entranceway to the walking trail started on the dew-covered grass but abruptly changed to a well-traveled dirt pathway through the dense, rain-soaked forest. Within a few minutes, the mud was replaced by sand as the oaks trees gave way to American beach grass and sand dunes. The sun reflected off the water, its subsequent glare not deterring or slowing our advance on one of Miles' favorite places, the beach.

He had grown to love the feeling of sand under his paws from the times we took him to the shore in Connecticut. We always assumed that Miles, who came from Kentucky, had never seen a beach or the ocean before. But it didn't take him long to learn that going to the land of sand meant long runs, playing fetch and lots of fun.

So when we went around the final turn at the end of the trail and passed through the dunes, Miles caught sight of the glistening water and openness of the beach.

He went nuts.

And all I did was encourage him as I threw the tennis ball, bouncing it along the coastline as he chased after it. It was only a matter of moments before 'devil dog' mode surfaced. He began to run this way and that way as he weaved between and around us in his version of an untouchable game of tag. He eventually settled down. Good thing no one was around because who knows what observers would have been thinking as they watched this unleashed, wild beast race around their quiet beach.

"Miles, you want to go in the water?" Sarah asked as she tossed the ball closer to the water's edge.

He paused.

"That's a no," I replied, as we watched Miles cautiously approach the floating tennis ball before retreating as the waves crashed in.

For Miles, this was a change of scenery from what he had grown accustomed to over the past year. The usual and expected tranquility of the sound at the beach in Connecticut was replaced by the crashing waves of the Atlantic Ocean in Cape

May. And it was clear. Miles didn't know what to make of those raised, moving walls of water.

We watched him play a game of cat and mouse with the ocean. As the water receded, Miles crept further out, leaving his sunken paw prints embedded in the soft, wet sand. That was only momentarily as he quickly retreated when the next round of waves crashed onto the shore. Given his breed, I figured he would be intrigued by the water, right? My thoughts were based on the notion that since he was part Labrador he would have some form of innate affinity for swimming and water.

Between each series of waves, Miles got closer and closer to the water. It was as if he was building a rapport, a unique trust with the approaching tide. At first, only the bottoms of his white paws would make contact with the darkened sand as he pranced on top of the receding tide. It wasn't before long that he was up to his ankles in the water, carefully treading along the coast while remaining mindful of the powerful current to his rear. And though he would race away from the impending crash, he trudged back in as the swells built in the background.

I was happy that he was enjoying himself.

"Look!," I eagerly pointed at Miles in the water. "Watch him Sarah! Watch him!" I laughed. Miles was biting at the water, taking in gulps of the sea as he plunged after tiny black minnows circling his paws in the shallows. Who knows what else he was going after as he snorted out the saltwater after dipping his nose into the blue. Moving sea shells, crabs, seaweed, all the above?

The light breeze from the west transitioned to a gusty wind. And in a short time, the bleak clouds approached from inland, negating the sunshine from earlier in the morning. Drops of rain began to fall, their countless indents on the ocean surface were clearly visible from afar.

And with that my curiosity as to whether he could swim would need to wait until another time as Sarah picked up his leash.

"It's going to rain bud. We'll come back, I promise," Sarah assured both of us.

Not wanting to be left behind, Miles raced towards the sound of his metal chain, completely forgetting his tennis ball on the water's edge. We quickly walked the length of the beach and headed back through the dunes towards the sand-coated path en route to our cottage.

Later that night, we took Miles into town and walked around before dinner. The come-and-go clouds had cleared, and that was more than a welcome sight after a couple of days of dreary skies. The silhouette of the Cape May Lighthouse was engulfed by the golden rays of the sun in the distance. There were probably a few dozen people who gathered on the beach and sidewalks to watch the sun set. The cool thing about this spot in Cape May is that you can see the sun rise in the morning on one side and set in the evening on the other, all from the same point. Once the sun fell below the horizon of the Atlantic, the temperature in the late September air followed suit. The cool ocean breeze reminded us that the warmth of summer would soon give way to the autumn colors of fall.

Miles hung out in the car as we indulged at The Pier, an elegant seafood restaurant with an amazing prix fixe menu that I will never forget. I don't think I ever ate more at any other point in my life than that night. This nine, yes nine, course meal was unbelievable, and in fact, it was more like thirteen courses for me as I ate what Sarah couldn't finish. The exemplary cuisine included braised pork ribs, seared ahi tuna, and cayenne-raspberry sorbet. Add on our favorite Riesling wine, and call it a night to remember.

Our vacation was going smoothly, but it wouldn't be complete if there wasn't an incident with our son. We had done everything right for the first two days, but we were bound to make a mistake as our comfort level increased. And we did. The next morning Sarah and I headed out to breakfast, leaving our furry friend at home. We had moved his crate into the bedroom, placed it under the window next to our bed, and positioned a fan in front of it to help keep him cool. When we returned home, we discovered bits and pieces of the white lace curtain that had once dangled from above the window in the bottom of his crate. The fan had blown the curtain through the grates, and Miles had unsurprisingly ripped it to shreds. He had also tore down the attached mounting from the wall when he pulled the delicate linen into his crate. Just great, I thought. Someone's going to need to tell Joanne.

For the next twenty minutes, Sarah searched the internet for curtain stores in Cape May, but the last thing I wanted to do on vacation was to go shopping for window draperies. Just add that $40 replacement to our final tab, I decided. Looking back, this wasn't Miles' fault. Or mine, if you get my drift. Wink wink.

On our last day of vacation, we drove up to Wildwood, a famous beach town just five minutes north of Cape May. The striking difference between the two towns was stark as it was easy to see that Wildwood was geared more to the bar-hopping, boardwalk-hanging, college-aged crowd while Cape May was meant for the ritzy, well-established, retirement community of South Jersey. That's why my dad preferred going down to Cape May, I realized.

Having said that, it was no longer the middle of July but the middle of September, and the town was empty, literally.

The hustle and bustle of summer was no more, as the quiet, empty boardwalk, which looked like it belonged in Cape May rather than Wildwood at the moment, spanned the coast of the Atlantic Ocean for over one mile.

Thinking it would be a good place to take Miles, we headed up the wood-planked ramp to the most famous boardwalk on the East Coast. The classic boardwalk game huts, local shops, and junk food stations were all boarded up and closed until next May. It was a cool morning as we strolled along, the chill in the air coming from the crossing oceanside breeze. An occasional runner or mother with a stroller would pass us as we trekked toward the deserted pier. Fortunately for Miles, we were able to sneak him on the boardwalk for a little bit of time, that was until a security officer approached us to remind us that dogs weren't allowed to be on there. I could almost guarantee that there were more rules, policies, and codes regarding dogs on the boardwalk than people based on all the signs I saw.

As we retreated off the walkway, the wind gusts off the water picked up in intensity, making the air temperature feel even cooler, so much so that we had to go back to the car to get sweatshirts before continuing our walk. But it wasn't before long that we meandered our way across the boardwalk onto the adjacent beach, which had, by far, the largest area of sand that I had ever seen. It must have been at least 200 yards wide. And we were literally the only ones walking on it. Yes, Miles was with us, and I'm sure that was yet another code violation.

There was an area on the beach where the water had pooled likely at the time of high tide. This man made oceanic basin was almost up to my knees as Miles trudged forward in full pursuit of a seagull. He raced back and forth in an attempt to catch one of these white birds, but he eventually realized he had no chance to catch these 'friends' as they soared over his head. By the way, that water was warmer than the air temperature, so maybe that's why Miles liked it.

Sarah, who was now wearing a white hooded sweatshirt, chased after Miles in an attempt to restrain him from going crazy as he uncontrollably raced after the seagulls. Her hair was crazy that day, which reinforced my memories of the gusty easterly winds. From afar, I watched the dark grey clouds slowly creep in across the ocean in the distance. The weather was soon gong to shorten our day yet again, so we picked up our sandals, and reversed course back towards the boardwalk.

Looking back at a text message I sent that day to my friend Dennis, I could only smile at my response when he asked what we were up to. Here is what I wrote:

"In Cape May for a few. Enjoying the warm weather and blue skies...I mean the 67 degree afternoon and rain."

And with that, we headed on home. Our first vacation with Miles was over. No injuries. No major problems. And definitely no beach weather. As Sarah veered onto the Parkway, the wipers were on yet again. Well, it was only appropriate as yet another thunder storm rolled in over the area.

And all I could think about were those text messages from my dad that I had read years earlier in the classrooms at the University of Connecticut. Maybe next time we'll share some of the great weather that my parents enjoyed during their trips.

CHAPTER 15

Training Day

"He listens to his trainer real good. He just doesn't listen to me. I still can't get him to do nothing."
— Evander Holyfield, on his Akita, who had completed obedience training with a professional trainer

We had tried it all. From shock collars to group training sessions, we spent hundreds and hundreds of dollars trying to solve Miles' behavioral problems in the first eight months.

So why stop at hundreds, when you can go to thousands?

Look, I'll be the first to say how difficult it was with Miles at the apartment. For a dog of his size and breed, there was no doubt he needed to' run free with the herd,' as my dad always says. Keeping him cooped up in a 1,000 square foot apartment was not ideal, but we didn't have many options. To make it even worse, when we went to work, he had to be in a crate. Otherwise the apartment would be unrecognizable. As a result, his anxiety grew worse as the daily separation continued to make him uncomfortable. The continuous barking, the 'devil dog' mode, the nipping at our heels when walking down the hallway as if we were being herded, the repetitive jumping and rambunctious nature never took a day off.

So when Sarah told me that she signed up Miles for an hour session with a company named Bark Stoppers, I was appreciative of her efforts to find the solution. Having said that, I was more than skeptical of the future outcome since the past results were subpar at best. And rightfully so. We spent a small fortune on classes, gadgets, and training books that I was hesitant to say 'yes' to dropping anymore money on a cause that seemed lost. I shook my head side to side, but then looked down at my forearm where the four scratch marks were engraved in my skin from earlier in the morning. I had gone outside to check the mail, and upon returning, Miles jumped up and latched onto my forearm with his nails. *Or were these from yesterday's incident*, I briefly asked myself.

"Alright maybe we can give it a try," I reluctantly gave into Sarah.

When she told me that that one hour session was going to be $300, I stared at her for a few seconds. Eyes wide open.

"I don't think the problems are that bad, are they?" I responded, clearly in sticker shock. Was this girl crazy? At that point, I was trying to pivot away from the conversation and did my best to shrug off Miles' behavior. What could possibly change Miles?

The check was in the mail the next day.

Border Collies are smart they say, but couldn't Miles have been just a little smarter and saved me a few hundred bucks by listening, oh I don't know, perhaps a few days ago?

One week later, I came home early on Thursday to see what was worth spending $300 on, or in my mind, $5.00 a minute. On the plus side, I couldn't wait to get out of work early. Anything to avoid staying at the hospital until 8:00 at night. Well, almost anything.

I arrived about ten minutes before the 2:00 afternoon session was about to begin. Sarah reiterated her desire for me to remain open-minded and positive with the meeting. I agreed with her. I wasn't going to dismiss the training session. Instead, I was going to try and make the most of it.

Knock knock.

"He's here, please be positive and pay attention," Sarah implored me, as she headed to the front door.

When the trainer from Bark Stoppers introduced himself, I couldn't help but stay focused, as his deep voice, vice grip handshake, and military-like presence commanded my attention from the start, despite the fact his thin frame belonged to a man in his mid-50s.

"Hello, I'm Keith," he started before stopping to push our jumping son off of his hip. "And this must be Miles," he smiled sternly at Sarah.

Oh boy Miles, this is real. It's happening. It's really happening. Good luck bud.

We broke the ice for a few minutes by talking about what we did for a living, how long he was with the company, and how his interest in this line of work came about. Then, we got down to business.

We sat down at the kitchen table where Keith began his presentation. He pulled out a three-ring binder containing page after page on the history of dogs. Each laminated leaf in that binder explored a different topic pertinent to what goes on in a dog's mind. Their social order and ranks. Who's the alpha male? Who's dominant, who's submissive, and what behavioral signs are associated with each. I tried to pretend that I was interested.

It was about fifteen minutes later when Keith directed his attention specifically on Miles. And his one-on-one session lasted about sixty seconds. I'm not kidding either.

Keith had asked us what one of our major problems with Miles was in the past few weeks. Sarah responded by telling him how he jumps on her when she comes home.

Learning of her concern, he asked Sarah to go outside the door and walk in like she would at any other point in time. And when she did just that, Miles unfortunately followed his typical pattern and jumped.

"BAH!" Keith barked, his gravelly voice grabbing the attention of all who were in the vicinity. The guttural sound reverberated throughout the hall. To say it was deafening would be an understatement. His introductory lesson may have bored me initially, but let me be clear, Keith had my undivided attention at this point.

And Miles' too.

Like the flip of a light switch, our furry friend became obedient, attentive, and submissive. He didn't jump, but instead sat down. His tail reversed course and curled between his legs and his eyes continued to glance back and forth between his mommy and daddy. He was beyond apprehensive. In fact, he looked scared.

"It's your turn," he told Sarah. "I want you to go outside, and if he jumps on you when you come inside, you 'bah' him." He gave Sarah a nickel-filled bean bag that she was instructed to throw down on the ground when Miles jumped. The goal was to have Miles associate the clinking, metallic sound with poor behavior and deter Miles from future transgressions whenever she picked it up. Unfortunately for Miles, he reared up on his back legs when Sarah returned from her brief departure, which opened the door to additional training.

"Baaah." Sarah's effort fell flat, as Miles appeared unfazed and behaviorally unchanged. I smirked as Keith remarked how Sarah's soft tone sounded more like a lamb than Miles' master. Oh, and she forgot to throw the bean bag down.

When our displeased trainer showed her how it should be done, the quick, abrasive tone shook Miles soul along with the apartment walls. Miles reverted back to his submissive posture, but this time he hurried off down the hall with his sunken tail curled underneath.

"Miles?" Sarah called from the living room. "Miles?" She tried again. But still no response.

We walked down the hall to find him cowering in the bathroom. Huddled in the far corner, Miles didn't move a muscle. His stare was sullen, his pupils were dilated, and his eyes glowed like a deer in the headlights. Even with his black coat, I could tell that his ears were pulled back, and I could hear him licking his lips as fear emanated from within.

He had enough for one day. His anxiety was palpable. Sarah tried to lure him with cookies and treats, but her efforts were met with an unforeseen resistance. He didn't even flinch at the sound of the cookie jar opening. I was amazed. This was the same dog that would be in a deep sleep down the hall with the bedroom door cracked, and just as you touch his box of Milkbones, you would expect to see his shadow next to you within seconds. That afternoon was the first time Miles ever declined an invitation for food.

"I think he's had enough for today," Keith informed us. *Thank you for that obvious statement,* I thought, as Miles remained coiled up in a ball on the bathroom rug.

Keith recapped the session and provided a quick overview of what he had achieved today. While I saw an immediate difference in Miles, two things came to my mind. For one, I was amazed at how the use of one word could bring about a 180 degree change in Miles so quickly. And two, did I just spend nearly $300 to learn that?

Whether or not the session would have a lasting impact was yet to be determined. As previously noted, we had tried all sorts of other options in the past, so I couldn't be too critical at that moment. But I couldn't help but think that Keith's training philosophy essentially boiled down to scaring the absolute shit out of your dog when he's at his most vulnerable and undisciplined point.

The last thing Keith told us was that some dogs will require an additional session in a couple of weeks to reinforce the principles and iron out any kinks that may arise.

"Another $300 Sarah! Are you kidding me? No way, no more," I stood my ground as Sarah closed the door after Keith left the apartment.

"It would only be $250 for a follow-up," Sarah noted. "We'll see how things go."

Without reading any more, you could guess who won that debate that night.

Three weeks later, there was a knock on the door, and Miles characteristically barked while he raced down the hall to investigate. He was scratching at the door and ready to pounce. But when Sarah opened the door, an all too familiar voice greeted her at the entranceway, and Miles abruptly retreated to the bathroom.

Keith had returned.

And all I could think about was the movie *Frankenstein* and how the doctor shouted out "it's alive, IT'S ALIVE!"

And I'm sure that in Miles' eyes, his version of Frankenstein was taller, more intimidating, and an even more imposing figure than he remembered.

The session focused primarily on fine-tuning what we learned a few weeks earlier along with how to have Miles walk disciplined while on a leash. We went through the expected routine by hitting the books inside before we took my glossy eyes outside to practice.

Sarah was pulled by the leash the instant she hooked it on Miles. And as Keith said in his own words, he would "have that addressed momentarily."

Uh oh, I gulped as I smiled nervously.

When Sarah handed the leash over to Keith, Miles stopped right in his tracks and couldn't help but stare at this daunting figure. His ears were perked and his focus did not deviate from his counterpart's face. Miles was so hesitant to take his eyes off of Keith that when they began to walk, his body went forward as his gaze was directed upward. The instant that Miles pushed ahead, I cringed with anticipation of what was about to come.

Keith's grip on the leash tightened in his hands as he pulled back on the reigns. Miles responded briefly, but when he again reverted back to his old behavior by darting ahead, that infamous word echoed in between the complexes' buildings.

"BAH!" He tugged firmly again on the leash and directed Miles to sit, which he did. *For your sake Miles, just do what the man says,* I pleaded internally. Even though it was a Friday afternoon, I didn't need any more attention brought to us outside the apartment by the trainer's booming voice.

And just like that, the session changed, as Miles no longer held his tail high and the inner anxiety had overcome his outward bravado. He was tentative to walk unless he was instructed to. He didn't leave Keith's side, or ours for that matter, for the rest of the walking session outside. It was like he was walking on egg shells, full of apprehension that the littlest of mistakes could trigger that fearful response.

Earlier in the afternoon, Keith had told us that when Miles pulled forward on the leash, that was his way of establishing dominance, almost as if he was the alpha male leading the pack. Well that status was no more as Miles gracefully paired up his gait to mine as we went step-by-step along the sidewalk and back into our apartment.

The session had ended. No follow-ups were planned. Thankfully.

Later that night, Sarah and I were having dinner when I looked below our glass top dining table to see Miles sleeping. He would usually be sitting next to Sarah or surveying the ground with the hopes that he would find a morsel of food or a fallen crumb. But tonight was different as he lay quiet asleep. It was yet another mentally exhausting day of training for our young pup. But he wasn't the only one thinking about the day.

I was hesitant to believe that Miles training would have a lasting impact.

The idea that we would randomly shout 'bah' and throw a nickel-filled bean bag on the ground whenever Miles did something wrong was unrealistic. It's one thing to do that in the privacy of your own home, but come on, who is honestly going to shout like a maniac in the middle of a park on a Saturday afternoon or at dinner on Christmas Eve. And if Sarah thought I was going to carry around that clanking bean bag wherever I went as if I were Linus holding onto my blanket, she had another thing coming.

Having said that, my mindset has evolved over the years, and to this day, I still use Keith's training tips. In fact, if Miles is not behaving well, I will simply look at him directly in the eyes and ask, "Do you want Keith to come back?"

But between me and you, I will always let Miles be Miles until Sarah starts to complain or threatens my wallet with more training sessions. To be honest, I think that I have trained him pretty well since that Thursday afternoon when Keith walked through our door. Now for Sarah on the other hand, I think Miles still has her trained, but I would never dare tell her that. I'm worried that she may have me write one more check for an additional session or perhaps sign me up for a new training class on yet another football Sunday in the fall.

CHAPTER 16

More Than Just a Dog

"A dog will teach you unconditional love. If you can have that in your life, things won't be too bad."
— Robert Wagner, actor in *The Longest Day*

My mom was sitting upright in her hospital bed as she struggled to find a comfortable position after her six hour back surgery. Shifting from side to side, she moaned at the slightest of movements. The intravenous lines remained in each arm as fluids and morphine steadily dripped from the raised stand above her headboard. The continual beeping from the monitor was the only constant as we all silently wondered what the future was going to look like in the weeks to come. Just hours out of surgery, my mom faded in and out of our talk, that is if you call mumbling words, incoherent speech, and a diminished attention span a conversation.

The lead up to that Tuesday in December had been a true reflection of my parents' lives. The ups and downs were paired with the trials and tribulations, all of which put a continuous strain on daily life for the past few months. The burden it had taken on my dad was visible. He had been taking care of my mom for almost a year. Grocery shopping, laundry, cooking, and arranging doctors' appointments became part of his normal weekly habit in addition to the daily routine of helping my mom get dressed and walk around the house. And if I need to remind you, all while working, planning his fast-approaching retirement and putting their house up for sale. It was almost like his full-time job was dwarfed by the around the clock position of homemaker and caretaker. Things had never come easy for my parents. With that in mind, it seemed like for every step backward, they took one and a half steps forward. They had always grinded their way forward, and this was going to be yet another time to put that to the test.

And there we were. My dad, brother, and I were sitting in my mom's post-op hospital room at Overlook Medical Center in Summit, NJ. It was just a handful of days before Christmas and a couple of weeks before the year 2015 was welcomed in.

I gazed out of the hospital room window. The snowflakes were falling down as the temperature followed their downward trend, coating the parking lot with a thin white blanket. This was not the winter wonderland my mom, or any of us for that matter, had in mind as we envisioned the upcoming holiday season. And though our conversation with my mom was limited, what she made clear was her concern that her spinal condition was going to ruin the fast approaching holiday.

Yes, this Christmas wasn't going to be like others in the past, but I knew that we had to stay positive and encouraging during this trying time. With that in mind, I was even more concerned about the overbearing burden on my dad's shoulders. There were not many things to smile about in recent weeks. So when Sarah called me later that evening from work to ask me how my mom was doing, I pivoted and rhetorically asked, 'how's my dad doing?'

It was now after nine in the evening, and my mom was sleeping in the bed so I decided it was time to leave. My dad was eating the meatloaf and mashed potato dinner that my mom had pushed away in disgust. My brother and I could only laugh as my dad chowed down. Nothing like hospital cuisine, especially if you haven't eaten all day, I figured. Being in a hospital, I'm pretty sure that meal cost $83.00. If I were my dad, I'd eat it too.

Walking outside was refreshing for obvious reasons. The winter cold was a welcomed change from the stale, warm air of the seventh floor. As I stepped foot into the frozen outdoors, the wind immediately whipped into my face. Although it was freezing, I paused and took a deep breath with the hope that the fresh air would clear my mind.

Fortunately, my car was parked in the garage a short walk from the hospital's main entrance. As I strutted along on the freshly fallen snow, I couldn't help but notice that it was like a sheet of ice on the underside. I called my dad to make him aware and to remind him to be careful; otherwise he may be my mom's roommate that night.

Opening my SUV door, I looked back to the welcomed sight of Miles bouncing around in the cargo area. A smile crossed my face. And though I would have loved to bring Miles in to the hospital to cheer up my mom, I knew that was not possible. *Or was it,* I grinned.

And that got me thinking.

In general, for someone that has never had a dog, one may look at this four-legged animal as a dependent creature that runs wild around the house as it sheds on the imported dining room throw rugs, drools on the kitchen tiles, scuffs up the oak wood floors, all while chewing on its owner's Coach bag or new work shoes. And though one may be right, I'm going to go on a little tangent here and tell you what else dogs are.

Dogs are genuine, loyal friends that provide a unique joy and an unbreakable devotion to their family. They don't lie or steal, unless it's a treat from the cookie jar. They don't scream or put others down. And unlike people, they wag their tails more than their tongues, and that in itself is a welcomed sight.

No, they don't pay taxes, but why should they as we already owe them our own debt of gratitude for the smiles they put on our face every morning we wake up and every evening we come home. Plus, all they ask for is a bowl of food, a walk, and a pat on the head. Imagine if everything in life was that easy. Sign me up.

Dogs are more than just running partners or home defenders, but walking buddies and kids' best friends.

In some cases, dogs protect our men and women on the battlefield. These warriors detect explosives, crawl through caves all while keeping a watchful eye. Yes, these military working dogs are soldiers. And they are veterans when they return home from their unselfish tours of duty and service. Truly amazing.

Dogs are a part of people's families, and in some cases, they are the only other member of that household. Till this day, I recall this old man who limped, cane in hand, into our veterinary hospital with his injured Doberman dog. Financially, this scraggly, stubble-faced retiree, who I had never seen before, appeared to have fallen on hard times as his soiled, ripped clothes and noticeable limp gave an insight into the personal struggles he had in his life at home. But rather than complain about the cost of the overnight emergency office visit, he looked me in the eye and said, "If my dog can't sleep at night, neither can I."

I will always remember that night more than most, even more so when I realized the reason he brought him in was simply for a broken toe nail. That Doberman was his family, and for whatever reason, I'm often reminded of it to this day.

So don't tell me that dogs are just dogs because until you have had one in your own life, that personal, indescribable connection cannot be appreciated.

With that in mind, I knew exactly what I was going to bring back to the hospital tomorrow for my mom.

Miles.

The next afternoon Sarah and I hopped into the car and took that forty-five minute drive back to the hospital with my mom's Christmas prize in the car. My mom unsurprisingly had a sleepless night. She was in pain. She didn't want to eat her breakfast. I wasn't surprised when my dad told me about the rough start to the day, as even she would admit that she was not the best of patients. She was in that all too familiar phase of post-operative depression as the realization of the long path to recovery had finally set in. Walking in, I figured that moment would be a good time to give my mom her Christmas surprise.

His open-mouth smile, long pink tongue, perky button ears, and stoic stance made for a great gift, as my mom unwrapped the portrait-like photo framed in a black painted wood frame with the words "Good Dog" written on the bottom. For the first time in a few weeks, I saw my mom smile. It was as if she had momentarily forgotten that she was in the hospital or that Christmas was next week.

Though I wish I could have brought Miles into her room, this was the next closest thing. I was certain that there couldn't have been a better Christmas gift, as this version of him would be allowed to reside with her throughout her stay at the hospital.

Later that night my dad called me up on his drive back to their house.

"Let me tell you son, when you gave Mom that picture, she was like a changed person, as if she got a little life back into herself." He went on to say that they shared stories about Miles for the rest of the night.

For the next three weeks, my mom split her recovery time between the hospital and the affiliated rehabilitation center. And over her shoulder, Miles looked down at her with that seemingly picture perfect smile of his. She asked about him every time we spoke including in early January when I stopped by for an afternoon visit.

"Your grandson has a new name. Murphy, Miles Murphy," I responded to my mom's inquiry as I looked at her with a wry expression.

Now you may be wondering where, or how, Miles earned his new middle name. To make a long story short, Miles was unsurprisingly out of control the previous weekend when we came home. He had left a trail of drool as he raced around the apartment with Sarah's shoe in his mouth, so I felt that it was time to restore order. So, I pretended to show great disappointment with him and the new name surprisingly rolled right off of my tongue. It was kind of like when a parent uses their child's full name to capture one's attention when something bad has happened.

I felt the goofy name with its alliteration was appropriate for more than one reason. And I could only imagine what Miles was thinking when he tilted his head while looking at me. *Why so many names dad?*

From that point on, it always made me smile when I used his full name because he was either doing something mischievous or overtly contemplating such behavior. And now, sitting in the rehab hospital, was as good of a time as any for a smile. My mom got a kick out of his new name, but her mind eventually transitioned back to her condition.

"I know that I need to stay here and get better," she reluctantly admitted to me one afternoon when I came to visit her in the rehabilitation hospital. "I just don't like not being able to do anything by myself." The realization of the limitations of her diminishing physical health, paired with the subsequent weight of dependency on others and the burden it placed on my dad throughout the past few years had set in while surrounded by the lonely isolation of room 415. For my mom, the mental and emotional complications brought on by her physical health restrictions were difficult to swallow, much more so than the countless vitamin D and calcium tablets of her morning routine that she had deemed to be the solution in years past.

"The days are so long here," my mom pointed out as the sterile silence echoed between the white walls of her room.

"Well you have Miles here with you," I noted as I pointed to his picture on the shelf.

"I know, I can't wait to see him again!" my mom's voice perked up as she went on to remind me how happy my dog was whenever she saw him back at the ranch.

Knowing that Miles wouldn't be allowed in the hospital, I made my mom aware of the pet therapy program offered at the rehabilitation center. I figured since Miles wouldn't be able to trot up to her room, then hopefully one of the hospital therapy dogs could pay her a visit. Sensing the need to change the conversation to something positive, I brought up wedding planning. I felt that if we could converse about anything other than her health, it would be beneficial for the both of us. Thus, we talked for a few minutes about the venue options, the guest list, and the menu tasting when there was a knock at the door.

"Sorry to interrupt you." The nurse was here to give my mom her afternoon medications as she pushed her drug cart into the room.

My mom would often introduce 'her son' to the nursing staff, and I didn't want to get locked down in another conversation with hospital staff so I decided now was the time to get going. Before I stepped out, I pointed at the picture of Miles next to her bedside.

"At least he's a good roommate," I joked as my mom began to talk to the nurse about her granddog.

In short, the days, weeks, and months that followed were not easy for my mom or my dad. For my dad, the onus of balancing her rehabilitation schedule and the demands at the home front while working and trying to set up meetings with the realtor was only complicated by that unfortunate lingering of my mom's health limitations.

Having said that, their external frowns turned upside down as their internal worries were in part alleviated whenever that characteristic knock on the front door was made. And though it was temporary, the relief and happiness that came when Miles Murphy stepped foot onto my parents' front porch was undeniable. Who could have ever imagined that a buoyant, fur-shedding, slobbering, long-nailed, four-legged animal who playfully ripped at my dad's forearm with his teeth while smearing his glasses with his tongue was capable of bringing such joy second only to his immediate family. And when he raced down the hallway to visit my mom, Miles slammed on the brakes and turned from devil-dog to angel as he brushed against my frail mother with a gentle touch. She was eager to pat his head and slip him a biscuit, all while balancing many a time with her cane close to her side but her furry friend even closer.

Miles still to this day has this unique ability to recognize the person before he interacts with him or her. While he may jump on Sarah or my dad whenever he has the opportunity, it's as if he has another sense when he is around my mom or even Sarah's grandmother. Sensing the frailty and recognizing his imposing power, he has always refrained from turning into that all too characteristic beast that I had grown to love, but instead a gentle giant that I learned to also appreciate.

Sure, the power of a dog's love can be explained to someone in words, but when that person is privileged to have that special emotional connection, the uniqueness of that experience will change their perspective on the value of a dog's devotion. Just ask that American soldier protecting our country overseas whose loyal four-legged comrade also patrols step by step with him in the desert sands of the Middle East. Or ask that old man who brought his Doberman into the veterinary hospital late at night because he couldn't sleep at night knowing that his only family member wasn't able to either. Or ask the young boy who can't wait to come from school to take his best friend outside for a walk or to even play fetch.

Or perhaps, ask my parents.

CHAPTER 17

LET IT SNOW

"The very fact of snow is such an amazement."
— Roger Ebert, American film critic and historian,
journalist, screenwriter, and author

There was something special about being a kid and watching the white flakes of snow pile up outside my bedroom window. For most of my childhood we lived in a two-story Colonial home surrounded on the outside by the vision of forest and the feel of nature. The backyard of the house was bordered by rows of evergreen and deciduous trees. The woodland was so dense that even from my bedroom window I could barely make out the often-traveled hiking trail weaving through the thicket. From the sight of deer to the sounds of nature, my observatory served its purpose at all times of the year, especially in the winter months. From my second-floor glass perch, I would watch the pine trees methodically become coated in the hue of white as the blades of grass in the backyard slowly faded below the accumulating precipitation. The contrast between the white of the snowflakes and the green of the evergreen foliage was negated with time as the colors blended together under the blanket of another December storm.

Winter had arrived.

And with the nippy frost, blustery winds, and frozen precipitation of the season came the thought that entered every student's mind. Was I going to have school?

As the anticipation built for the approaching storm, I was always amazed by the same feeling that I felt every time the meteorologist called for accumulating precipitation. The novelty of a winter storm never wore off as I looked forward to strapping on my boots, shoveling the driveway, and building snow forts as tall as the mailbox. However, I cannot leave out the other important factor. The thought of having a delayed opening, an early dismissal, or perhaps a three day weekend entered my mind immediately, especially when the snow started early enough on a Thursday afternoon. I recall how I would continue to look at the deck railings to see whether or not the snow piling up had crossed that magical, gut-feeling threshold to close school. Every storm, every year. It never changed.

I didn't just have that mindset about winter in my elementary school years. In fact, I had a similar feeling when I was in college and even veterinary school, for there was something undeniably magical that came with the onset of a winter snowstorm.

The freshness of the cold winter air paired with the subtle sound of snowflakes falling from the clouds always rekindled my memories of the season from years past. My recollection of looking outside the window in the morning after a night filled with weather reports and anticipation was something that I had grown accustomed to by living in the Northeast for most of my life.

So when we had our first major winter storm in January 2014, my thoughts quickly pivoted to Miles Murphy, as I understandably was intrigued with how he would handle the change of scenery.

Having lived in Kentucky, we thought that Miles was more likely to have seen a tornado than snow in his brief time in the Southeast. Now I'm sure there may have been the occasional flurry or snow shower, but to think that it would amount, literally and figuratively, to the totals expected for a northeastern winter was unlikely.

Following the same pattern from my academic years, I rolled out of bed on that January morning to see for myself if the predictions made by the weather prognosticators had come true. Boy, did they ever. At least five inches of pure white fluffy snow had fallen the night before as I looked out at the porch railings and car roofs to judge the total. Snow was continuing to fall heavily from grey skies as the northwest wind carried it diagonally in front of our window.

"Miles, guess what!" I shouted across the room as I opened my palms out to my sides. He lifted his head abruptly, startled by my unusual, early morning energetic tone. "It snowed! It snowed!"

And with that he tilted his head and lunged off of the bed, his anticipation flowing through his veins. He was only excited because of the tone of my voice, not because of the weather outside. The word 'snow' was not yet a part of his vocabulary, but we were well aware that was going to change in the near future.

"Come look in the window," Sarah suggested, pointing at the sliding door. Recognizing that word and routine, Miles raced over and poked his nose in between the vertical blinds to investigate what Sarah was pointing at. His intrigue and curiosity turned to confusion as his nose remained plastered against the window while his eyes darted from side to side. He quickly looked back at his mother as if he were saying 'what is this stuff?'

Leashed and ready to be unleashed, Miles flew around the corner at the instant our apartment door cracked open. He tore the leash out of my hand, and from that point on, it was an all-out sprint down the hallway, his curiosity leading him in leaps and bounds towards the exit while I chased after him. His excitement was barely containable as he ran around in a circle with the handle of the leash held squarely in the clench of his jaws. I struggled to gain back control of the leash as he began to hop at the door. His paw prints were all over the adjacent walls. I could only shake my head as I pushed open the frozen glass door to the outside.

And just like that, he stopped.

I couldn't believe it. It was as if I had flipped a switch and converted his excitement from the inside into a solemn focus outside. Miles stood there, extending his neck forward as he sniffed the cold January air while watching individual snowflakes float in front of his eyes. Hesitant to move forward, he placed his paw gingerly into the frozen white landscape. He pulled it back, but not before leaving his paw print forged into the once fluffy powder. This was a lot different than the open sidewalks and grassy areas that he had grown accustomed to over the past six months. I'm sure he was thinking that just a handful of hours ago his home looked a whole lot different.

Miles' black coat was now speckled with these tiny white flecks. For a good minute, he didn't move a muscle, but just stood there and watched the scenic changes unfolding before his eyes. It wasn't before long that the snow gave the illusion that the coat on the top of his body was white with a black underbelly.

He remained frozen in place as the snow picked up in intensity. For a dog that was going crazy just a few minutes earlier and wanted to be the first to race outside, I was amazed how our alpha male dog suddenly sank to the back of the pack.

"Let's go Miles," I said, looking at Sarah in disbelief. I gave a quick tug on the leash and stepped forward into the ankle-deep snow. I guess his family's reassurance was all he needed as he followed suit and plowed forward through the snow As we walked ahead, Miles burrowed his muzzle under the snow to take in all the different smells, but just far enough not to compromise his watchful eye on the pathway from above the snowfall's horizon. Every few seconds, Miles would bring his entire head above the surface to spray the accumulated snow now out from his nostrils. He always had the colors of a killer whale, and now it seemed like he had the actions of a blow hole as well.

With every step we took along the pathways, Miles sniffed and prodded his way through the snow as if he were trying to discover something hidden underneath. But the emptiness of his discovery only provided more fuel for his curiosity as his intrigue with the winter weather increased. Though the overnight storm would not be considered a blizzard, it did introduce Miles to the tidings of winter by giving him a taste, literally and figuratively, of the snow that the season has to offer.

As the weeks and months moved along, Miles looked increasingly forward to his winter walks and the sight of snow as the weather patterns and elements became a routine part of everyday life. It didn't take long for him to recognize the unique changes of having four distinct seasons in the northeast as his time in Kentucky was simply now just a memory. Even at night, the frigid air would not cool his longing for a late evening stroll. It's almost as if he embraced the cold temperatures and the associated challenges that came with the weather.

For the next couple of months, Miles became accustomed to the snow that fell during the winter months. A few inches today, a couple of inches the following week, six inches the next month. The winter storms that dropped their characteristic white precipitation never failed to lose Miles' interest and always left a manageable blanket of snow that would keep him entertained for the weeks ahead.

Well that changed, albeit briefly, in January 2015 when Miles awoke to a snowstorm that only his dreams could envision.

When Miles walked outside the door, like we had done hundreds of times over the past couple of months, he stopped. His eyes did a double take and eagerly looked around. He glanced up at me before shifting his focus over to Sarah. His hesitancy was tangible. The snow was blowing sideways in the wind, forming knee high drifts in the corner of our patio. It was nearly a foot high and unofficially touched his chest as I leaned over to draw an imaginary line across the white peak staring at Miles from ahead. *So much for those three inch snow totals,* I thought to myself as I rubbed his head in reassurance.

To put it into perspective, picture walking outside your front door to find the snow up to your waist. I couldn't blame Miles that he was hesitant to take another step forward. I couldn't even make out the steps that were buried in snow, so imagine what Miles was thinking.

"It's cold Miles!" Sarah remarked as I saw my warm breath frozen the instant it touched the icy air. My skin tingled as the left side of my face continued to be softly pelted with the downfall of snowflakes. But fortunately, the snow was light as I made my way towards the steps. Using my snow boots, I dragged the bottom of my soles along the frozen concrete steps and easily cleared the path of the fluffy snow. It blew away in the gusty wind, revealing a walkway that our dog was accustomed to seeing.

And with that, Miles took off from the top step and soared into the snow. Not caring that it was up past his chest at certain points, he jumped and vaulted his way down the snow-covered sidewalk as he relied on his memory of the surrounding area. It was still early in the morning so the apartment crew had not yet started the unenviable task of shoveling the narrow walkways or plowing the crowded streets, but that was okay, because I think Miles was enjoying the challenge of navigating around the snow course. In fact, I don't know who was enjoying it more as we playfully jogged along the pathway that we felt was the sidewalk. As we turned the corner along the side of the apartment, I told Miles to wait as Sarah continued her trek ahead. Being away from his mother, Miles began to whine and grow impatient as he watched Sarah stop in her tracks. She turned around and stared back at him in his direction.

"Wait, waaait," I whispered as I felt the energy and excitement begin to boil inside of our fireball on this frozen morning. Now sitting, his whimper grew louder as he adjusted the positioning of his front paws, one after the other, ensuring he could get the most traction on the slippery, snow covered pathway. His forward stare never deviated, as his focus remained solely on the eyes peering back at him from thirty feet in the distance.

"Ready, go!" I shouted as I released my hold on his collar. His athleticism was on full display as he darted through the snow, clearing a path forward before leaping into the air with his final bound at my expectedly hunkered-down fiancé, who quickly pointed towards me. A sudden stop was followed by a quick pivot before Miles continued his enthusiastic run, this time in my direction.

"Devil dog! Devil dog!" I blurted out with a giddy smile as our rambunctious, fearless dog raced towards me, his legs moving faster than the rest of his body. He circled tightly behind the back of my knees before heading back to Sarah in the third and final lap of his morning sprint.

His muzzle was now completely white as he blinked his brown eyes around his snow-covered face. And it didn't seem to bother him at all. In fact, I think he was in his glory and on such an adrenaline rush that he wouldn't have cared if the snow was twice as deep. It seemed like he could run around all day outside and not be fazed by the blizzard conditions.

All in all, over twenty-three inches of snow fell in our area over the course of seventy-two hours. The mounds of snow that were formed by plowing the streets were topped off by the piles shoveled from the adjacent sidewalks, reaching a height of over five feet in certain areas. The temperatures remained frosty in the weeks ahead and no one was happier than the adventurous Mr. Murphy, who enjoyed climbing these frozen, manmade ice mountains. Rather than walk on the cleared, de-iced sidewalks, he'd prefer the unconventional challenge of hiking across the snow-covered grass. The digits on his paws were splayed out with each nail struggling to make an indent in the frozen snow as he clawed his way along the slippery surface. The sound of his nails scraping the icy top of the snow sent chills down my spine, even more so when the angle of the snow pile grew steeper. Though I worried at first how Miles would handle the snow, I quickly learned that our daring son was up for the challenge and looked forward to taking it on. The only thing that was difficult for Miles was finding a spot to go to the bathroom, but I don't think he minded the compromise.

As is the case every year, there was the eventual transition from the cold bluster of winter to the vibrant warming of spring. I always wondered what went on in his mind, if he even thought about the weather, the changing temperatures, the revolving weather patterns.

It's fun to speculate, but I'm pretty certain he knows when a new season is coming. Miles enjoys all times of the year, but there is definitely something special about the winter. I like to look at it through his eyes and the unique, worry-free perspective that he shares. Perhaps it's the novelty of the snow or the tracking of an animal's foot prints along a trail that goes hand in hand with the freshness of the air and the fact that there is no suffocating summer-like humidity. Or maybe it's the challenging climbs up a slick snow bank at the site that was previously a straight paved pathway covered in leaves in the fall or lined by blooming flower buds in the spring.

While parents are concerned about school closings and slippery roads, children worry whether there will be enough snow to sled down their backyard hills on their days off. But even though there are such instances where the thoughts and feelings towards the winter weather conditions may vary, there is that undeniable amazement that comes with a snowstorm. It's an attraction that has the capability of drawing the attention of anyone of any age, from the baby-faced adolescent to the young at heart retiree to even our four-legged furry friends. Year after year, this amazing sight lures us all to our familiar perch where we press our noses against the same glass paned window from years past and stare with our ever watchful eyes focused, perhaps for different reasons, on the pine trees, lawns, sidewalks, and rooftops as they turn to white.

In the words of J.B. Priestley, "The first fall of snow is not only an event, it is a magical event. You go to bed in one kind of a world and wake up in another quite different, and if this is not enchantment, where is it to be found?"

It just so happens that for many of us, including Miles Murphy, every snowfall brings the same delight as that first snowfall.

CHAPTER 18

The Best Dog

"Dogs are not our whole life, but
they make our lives whole."
-Roger Caras, photographer and writer

It was definitely one of the most memorable phone calls that I ever made in my life. So many thoughts and memories were racing around my mind as butterflies fluttered in my stomach. It was the day that I had thought about for quite some time. I'll never forget that June afternoon.

"Hey Phil," Sarah's mom answered the phone at the other end. Mrs. Aupperlee is what I still call her to this day. We talked for about ten minutes about our jobs, the end of her elementary school year, the approaching summer, and small things like that. It felt like a normal conversation because I wasn't thinking about anything. But when it dawned on me that I was going to ask for her blessing and her daughter's hand in marriage, it felt like I had an anaphylactic reaction as my throat seemingly narrowed, and I struggled to get the words out. But I did.

And that was supposed to be the easy phone call, as my thoughts transitioned to calling her father next.

At that point, Sarah had been my best friend for nearly the past ten years. We did everything together dating back to our years at the University of Connecticut. From dining hall dinners to UConn basketball games, we had a great time in the four plus years that we shared together in school. As we made the most of the next four years spent apart when I was out in Oklahoma, we shared dinners and watched movies, all via that streaming online video chat. Long before we began to live together in New Jersey, I knew. And it had all come to fruition.

Miles had traveled the state with me from August 2013 to June 2014 as we paired up in search of that prized jewel. I would tell Sarah that we would be going to the park or that I would be going to the gym, when in reality, I was visiting different jewelers in the area. There was that one really late Saturday night that I told Sarah work had kept me longer than the norm. I figured that she would believe me since every night I would seemingly work late. All in all, I definitely enjoyed the nearly yearlong search. It was important to me. In fact, I have still held on to all of the business cards that I accumulated over that period of time.

On the afternoon of August 18, 2014, we left Miles with his grandma in East Lyme, CT and headed up to UConn for what Sarah thought was going to simply be a walk down memory lane in the small town of Storrs. As we strolled around the campus, we reminisced on our memories as we passed each site. Sarah knew exactly where we were when we sat down on a wood bench in what we called the 'secret garden,' a secluded, grassy area on the outskirts of campus that was surrounded by a wall of trees but filled with the tranquil sounds of a fountain that steadily dripped water. Sitting next to Sarah on the bench, I talked about the importance of having her in my life and being by my side as my best friend for the past decade. And it wasn't before long that I dropped down to one knee and proposed to the best person in the world. She said 'yes,' of course, otherwise I wouldn't be talking about it at all in this chapter. From that point on, it was as if I were floating on cloud nine. For the rest of the afternoon we walked around the center of campus with smiles on our faces before heading back to East Lyme for dinner.

It took use nearly an hour to get back to Sarah's mother's home, which gave me plenty of time to reflect on the day. Mrs. Aupperlee knew that Monday afternoon in August was going to be the big day, but she waited for Sarah to break the news before saying anything just in case there was a change of plans in our day. And you guessed it, Miles was jumping up and down when the cheers came from the kitchen.

For the next six months, Miles voyaged around with us as we visited different wedding venues, florists, caterers, and vendors. And every time we walked into a new wedding venue, Sarah would always ask, "Is our dog allowed to be in the wedding?"

From the start, Sarah had made it very clear to me that she did not think spending a hot summer afternoon at UConn taking our engagement photos with Miles was a good idea. She felt that it would be too much for Miles to handle in addition to the fact that he wouldn't be allowed to go inside some of the buildings during our session. Hence, we agreed that if he wasn't going to be in those photos, he would have to be in the ones taken at the wedding ceremony. Thus, the venue needed to allow our dog otherwise we would be on the search for another location to celebrate our wedding.

Man, I was so happy with that pact. Through my eyes, it was like when the Boston Red Sox traded some guy named Babe Ruth to the New York Yankees for $25,000 in 1920 or when the United States acquired a meager 827,000 square miles of land west of the Mississippi River from France for just $15 million in 1803. Like the Yankees and the United States, I definitely felt like I got the better end of that deal.

Through my eyes, I would have had regrets if I didn't have Miles in the wedding. Over the past years, this dog traveled everywhere with us. From our vacation in Cape May to the journey down the street to the grocery store, Miles has honestly been in our car at least twice a day and has gone wherever we went. And on the biggest day of our lives, I couldn't leave him in a kennel. With that in mind, there were some obvious concerns. First off, his barking. Need I say more? And second, his jumping. Secretly at night, I prayed that he wouldn't characteristically place his dirty paws on Sarah's wedding dress until after the ceremony. For his sake and mine. With all of the wedding photos to be taken, the last thing we needed was to have brown paw prints plastered on Sarah's dress.

November 6, 2015. Waking up in my hotel room on the morning of our wedding day seems as clear as ever to me. Even though the clock read 5:30 AM, I was wide awake and excited but full of nervous anticipation for the day ahead of me. I never liked to be the center of attention, but I felt that my better half would fortunately take that spotlight away from me later that day. After I rolled out of bed, I finished writing Sarah's card, and before I wrapped her gift, a photo book recapping the past ten years, I flipped through the pages yet again.

In the back of my mind, I couldn't believe how fast the past decade flew by. From our first pictures to our first vacation to our first dog, I was happy with the past, yet excited for the future. When I saw the two pages dedicated to Miles, I transitioned my thoughts to him. I knew that if my mind couldn't relax and allow me the simple pleasure of a good night's rest on my pillow top mattress king-sized bed in my luxurious two-room suite, then I was all but certain that Miles' night spent on the cold cement, in what I referred to as solitary confinement in the kennel, was way worse than mine.

For me, there's nothing worse than dead time where I just sit around because it allows my mind to churn and think and churn some more. So I was happy that within an hour I was going to be driving the fairways of the Lymand Orchards Golf Course. As I put the final bow on the gift, I got into my black golf collared shirt and tan khakis before heading down to the lobby.

Sarah's brother Scott and her Uncle Bob joined me for our morning round. Let me tell you, driving in a golf cart with Scott would make you want to have either seat belts installed in those things or even make you consider walking with a pull cart instead. I'm sure the cart was at a forty degree angle when we cruised over the hills on the seventh fairway. Playing with Scott was fun because he made me feel at home when he hooked his third consecutive drive on the eighth hole into the pine trees. With that in mind, he definitely hit the ball better than me. Uncle Bob put us both to shame. This Florida resident plays golf a couple of times a week so I'm sure that helped explain his birdies on four holes on the front nine. He told some good stories when we played with him. And I'm not talking about 'when I was a young boy' types of tales, but funny jokes and inappropriate stories that even Sarah chuckled at when I repeated them. His good nature and witty personality helped me relax on that cloudy New England morning, and I appreciated his mentality of giving me the benefit of the doubt when it came to putting for my birdie attempts by picking up my ball and saying, "It's your wedding day. You were going to make it anyway."

Even without the assistance, I played the best round of golf of my life.

When we made our way back to the hotel, I showered and got dressed into my blue suit, white pressed dress shirt, tan dress shoes, polka dot blue tie. I accessorized my look with a white pocket square and a wrist watch that Sarah had gifted to me. I had never been into style or clothes, but I truly enjoyed getting dressed that late morning.

"I need you there for 1:00 in the afternoon," was the second to last thing Sarah had asked me as we said our good-byes the night before following the rehearsal dinner. "Don't be late" was the last thing. And when I showed up at the Barns of Wesleyan Hills ten minutes after one, I was bracing for a disappointed bride, but it turned out that she wasn't even ready herself. At least that's what Amy, our wedding planner, had told me when I arrived. For all I know Sarah could have been angrily flipping tables over on the inside of those barn walls, but Amy kept me calm.

Due to the time of year, we decided to have a 'first look' and all of our pictures taken before the ceremony to ensure there was good lighting. Well, the weather on that nearly seventy degree November afternoon didn't let us down as the autumn sunshine illuminated Sarah's already luminous look. The sight of her in her strapless, lace-lined, fit and flare wedding dress paired with her bright smile reminded me that I was the luckiest guy in the world.

Not before long, our son arrived at the venue for his long awaited appearance. His personal driver, a family friend, nicely escorted him from the kennel where he had stayed the night before. Sarah is the first to remind me how complicated it was to not only arrange Miles transportation from and to the kennel, but to get him accepted into the kennel. Besides needing additional vaccines, Miles needed to attend daycare at the camp for a one-on-one interview with the staff in the weeks prior to the wedding to determine if he could get along with other dogs. He passed the initial evaluation, earned a certificate for good behavior, and most importantly, was accepted into the daycare program. Phew.

While we gathered in the suite with our wedding party before the beginning of the ceremony, Miles did his best to simultaneously keep my pre-vow nerves at ease on one side while pushing the limits on the other.

As I sat down on the leather couch for a moment to gather my thoughts, Miles came around the corner and nudged his face underneath my hands as he sought my attention. He sat in front me and his tail began to wag as if he was saying, "You're going to be great, Dad!" Or at least that's what I remember telling myself. I'm sure he was actually thinking about when his next treat was going to come or when he could make his move at the cheese and cracker station across the room.

Well, his tranquility came to an abrupt end when Sarah entered the room. He quickly became overwhelmed, and he began to bark at the sight of his mother. I could not break or give in, even as the piercing noise ricocheted inside the wood-walled room. Sarah had specific instructions to not let Miles near her until after the ceremony. That's like trying to tell a wolf to stay away from raw meat that is just steps away. Of course, I had the unenviable job of fulfilling my bride's request.

"This is not a good start," I shouted at Sarah across the room as I tried to calm him down. I knew going into that day that Miles' patience was going to be pushed to its limit. I just didn't know it was going to start that soon.

Not before long he had overturned his water bowl when running around the room. And of course, he had to make his presence known with a little game of tug-of-war using the paper plates from the cheese and cracker station. Wrong time, wrong place Miles Murphy.

Recognizing that I was in distress, Sarah finally came over to appease our high-strung dog and to help quiet him down. Sitting in front of his mother, Miles excitement began to fade. With my focus no longer being on our dog, I looked out through the multi-paned glass window and saw our hotel shuttle bus arrive. Our guests had arrived. Actually, many were already sitting in their seats as the bus emptied the last of the arrivals.

I began to think about the past ten years while checking for the nth time that my vows were in my suit pocket. Standing in a room of family and friends did little to help calm my nerves, as I longed to just have some time alone to gather my thoughts and myself. It had finally hit me that I was getting married. An anxious anticipation began to brew on my insides. My palms were beyond moist, but more like dripping wet. My stomach felt like it was doing its best to turn inside out. My heart was racing. With that said, I did my best to casually play things off to an ever-observant outside world.

"It's time to get lined up," Amy announced as she walked into the bridal party suite. "We're going to start in a few minutes," she said as she spoke into her headset.

Miles was happy to go anywhere as Scott walked him around the parking lot to alleviate his energy. We all knew how Miles could get when he's in a new setting and around new people.

Besides jumping on her dress, Sarah's second big concern was how Miles would handle the ceremony. Was he going to bark? How would he handle the fact that his mother was going to be twenty feet away from him? Sarah already had an escape plan for her nephews Ian and Jasper if they were to begin to cry, so it wasn't surprising to learn that she had a family friend waiting on the edge of the aisle to whisk Miles away if he began to bark at any point during the ceremony.

But I wasn't concerned, for I could attest to the power of the all mighty peanut butter stuffed bone. I've seen its magic on Christmas Eve, Thanksgiving, and other crowded, chaotic holiday settings when it held its own against the tempting aromas and luring flavors of roasted prime rib, ham, and turkey. The key to having serenity on, let's say a Christmas holiday, was to give Miles a new bone. As a veterinarian, it was only natural that I worried about the wear and tear that the bone would have on Miles' teeth. But as a guest at someone's house for a holiday, I worried about not being asked to come back to next year's celebration.

Need I say more, as this November 6th was my wedding day, and I was not going to take any chances. I handed Scott a new, fully stuffed, peanut butter bone with the simple, straightforward instruction to 'give him the bone'. End of story.

As the processional music began to play my parents made their way down the aisle. I took great solace in seeing them walk arm in arm after the challenges they faced in recent years. I took a quick look at the rest of the outdoor arrangement. There were about eight rows of white chairs lined up on both sides of the processional walkway. A willow tree across the creek filled the backdrop as the golden and orange tree leaves scattered on the grass provided us a subtle reminder of the season and the aesthetic feeling of a rustic fall wedding.

When Bruno Mars song "Marry You" played in the background, that was our cue to head out as Scott and Miles joined me along the couple hundred-yard stroll from the barn down to the faux-altar. What an amazing walk to share with my brother-in-law and son. I laugh as I think back to that moment and watch the videos over and over from our wedding. Miles was looking stellar as ever. We had given him a bath two days earlier and his coat shined in the glow of the afternoon sun. His navy blue harness matched our color scheme and his matching white-striped bow tie added some elegance to our underdressed family member. May I remind you that he was a part of our wedding party. His title: Groomsdog. The white tip of his tail pointed to the sky as he wagged it ever so graciously back and forth. It looked like he was smiling as he pranced down the pathway. Except for the occasional deviation from the path or the sporadic sniff, Miles remained fairly disciplined along his walk down. His curiosity was on full display as he led Scott down the aisle. He was darting from one side of the walkway to the next, his nose taking in the wide range of smells found along the processional trail. Except for the sole stop midway to mark his territory, Miles managed the walk better than expected.

But I was not going to push the limits, especially at this time. With Sarah soon to be on her way down the aisle, I had told Scott to give Miles whatever treats he had if our son needed a distraction. With the help of the peanut butter bone, I didn't think about Miles until the ceremony concluded. There was no barking, no whimpering, no growling, but only silence from his side. And with that, my focus shifted towards my soon-to-be bride.

The best part about the long walk from the barn was the fact that I could relish the sight of Sarah walking arm in arm with her dad for that much longer. As Billy Joel's "She's Got a Way" played, I soaked in the sounds and appreciated the scene as I thought about what I was going to say in my vows.

As the ceremony progressed, Sarah and I shared our hand-written personal vows with one another. Mine were written like a story that recapped the past decade in time, beginning with the first class we attended together at UConn.

Sarah wrote her vows in the form of a poem, and even gave our dog some recognition with the line, "...You take care of Miles when he is sick, and you help me with my fantasy football picks."

When the ceremony concluded, all bets were off as Sarah finally agreed to take a family picture with Miles. Yes, our dog. And yes, while wearing her wedding dress. I was surprised at first, but took advantage of the opportunity as I called our photographer Matt over for the prized picture. The image of me squatting down to the right of Miles with Sarah leaning in over his opposite shoulder is one of my favorites, and we have it framed on our mantle where we can look at it every day.

And sooner than desired, the natural light in the sky began to fade. Sarah and I headed off into the barn for the reception and to dance the night away. That was not without first saying good night to our son, who would be spending the rest of the evening at the kennel. Even though Amy and the venue welcomed our dog and said he could stay, we both agreed that we didn't want to push our luck. With that, Miles was driven back by our family friend to the same kennel for yet another lonesome evening after a fun-filled afternoon with his friends and family.

People always have something to say, and looking back at our wedding, I am happy that I didn't listen to others who recommended that Miles not be a part of our big day. It seemed only fitting that for the dog that wants to be around us all day, every day that we justifiably returned the favor by including him in our biggest day. And while others floated their concerns about him jumping on a dress or barking during the ceremony, or this or that, my greatest concern was having that lifelong regret that Mr. Miles Murphy wasn't a part of *our* day.

Oh, by the way, Sarah and I have no regrets having Miles at the wedding.

In less than two days, we were to head off on our honeymoon down to St. Lucia, and unfortunately the resort didn't allow dogs. Because our flight from John F Kennedy airport was departing early in the morning, we had to say goodbye to Miles the night before.

Walking around the grass on the outside of the kennel, all I could focus on were the howls, woofs, and yaps from within. The sounds blended together to form an almost deafening racket as we proceeded ahead. I'm sure it didn't help Miles' nerves. Perhaps that explained why he began to whimper and pace around the lobby. As usual, he was tentative at first but once he joined his friends in the playpen, I could rest a bit as I watched him interact with the others on the lobby television screen. It still felt like dropping your kid off at school for the first time. That was tough for me. It was the first time that we were leaving Miles for more than a day.

The next morning, we flew out from New York en route to our honeymoon and our first vacation in years. Having never been to the Caribbean before, I was amazed at the clarity of the turquoise water and the smoothness of the pale white sand. I told Sarah that it reminded me of the Jersey shore, in the sense that there was sand and water. "That's where the similarities end," she replied slyly.

It was difficult for me to not think about Miles. For one, part of my daily routine focused on our dog. From walks to meals to even sharing the bed, Miles had been a part of our everyday lives for more than two years. It was almost as if it was built into our minds as a way of life. To wake up one morning 2,500 miles away and not have to measure one and a half cups of his kibble for breakfast was unusual. Sounds crazy to think about when you're in the eighty-five degree Caribbean sunshine, but I missed the daily duties that I had grown accustomed to doing for the past thirty months. Throughout our ten day stay, the smallest of things like the sight of a stray dog jogged my memory of our furry friend. Every day we spent some time watching the live web cam of Mr. Miles Murphy as he ran around camp with his friends.

But we did that all while sitting in beach chairs and sipping our mixed drinks in front of the calm waters of the Caribbean Ocean.

There's a saying that all good things must come to an end, and sorry to say, our trip in paradise followed suit. Fortunately for Miles, Mrs. Aupperlee had rescued him from his stay at the kennel about halfway through our trip. She told us that when they arrived back at her house, he slept for the next two days. I'm convinced that he doesn't sleep at daycare. Having said that, when we walked through the front door, Miles appeared well rested, and he made up for lost time as he couldn't hold himself together. He was so excited to see his family that he could not stop himself from jumping off the ground and prancing around the floor in devil dog mode. And this was at midnight. But I understood. For Miles, it must have felt like a month since he last saw his family. To be honest, he wasn't the only one with those feelings.

CHAPTER 19

The Harness

*"It is scarcely possible to doubt that the love of man has
become instinctive in the dog."*
— Charles Darwin, English naturalist and geologist

April 28, 2016.

"Miles is coughing," Sarah said in a panic over the phone as
she called me first thing in the morning from Connecticut. In
the background I could hear a dry, raspy cough continue for
about ten seconds.

Because I was still working in New Jersey, I couldn't see
Miles, let alone examine him. Initially, I thought that Miles
had something in the back of his throat, so I suggested that
Sarah give him some peanut butter to help soothe the back
of his throat, kind of like a lozenge. But when the coughing
episode started up again, I knew that he had kennel cough,
a highly contagious upper respiratory tract infection that he
likely obtained from one of his playmates at camp last week.

Anyone that puts their dog in daycare knows that there is
always a risk. It's almost like sending your son or daughter to
first grade. It's more surprising if they don't get strep throat or
an ear infection over the course of the school year than if they
do. Given the fact that Miles and the other dogs share water
bowls, rub noses, and interact within inches of each other's
faces, I was surprised that Miles didn't end up with kennel
cough sooner. Even though he was up to date on his vaccines,
there are many other viruses out there that can contribute to

the condition. He was just unfortunate to have been exposed to one of them.

His coughing episodes were bad, as Sarah showed me on our video chat later that evening. He would often stop dead in his tracks, crouch down, and cough, sometimes even bringing up white phlegm. Any pressure on his throat, or more specifically his trachea, would trigger that hacking response. Oh, and so would excitement, but that was impossible to contain.

Sarah was spending a few days at her mother's house before we moved from New Jersey. Being in a different location, it was all but guaranteed that Miles would go into his coughing fit, especially when someone new walked by outside. At that point, his excitement would be too much to handle. As a veterinarian, I felt that supportive care at home was all he needed. Fortunately for Miles, nurse Sarah was there to comfort him. He was eating, energetic, alert, all while not showing any advanced signs of a progressive illness. In other words, the body along with the helping hand of time would take care of this viral condition. The only thing I recommended was to take off his collar and replace it with his harness so that his throat wouldn't become irritated when he pulled on the leash during his walks.

Little did I know that putting the harness on him would nearly turn into a $5,000 fiasco.

April 29, 2016.

I quickly learned that when Sarah calls me early in the morning, it usually isn't for a casual chat. When she calls me at work, that's an 'uh oh' moment. And when Sarah starts a conversation off with "Miles is doing fine, but we have a little situation," I know that little situation is in reality a whole lot bigger.

"Miles ate part of his harness," she continued on the other end of the line. I threw my arms up in the air as I began to talk to myself as the voice on the other end of the line carried on. *How could this happen*, I asked.

It turned out that Sarah and her mom had left Miles in his crate when they stepped out of the house. The only problem was that he still had his harness on.

By now, I had logged onto our video chat to see the damage.

"He chewed it off," Sarah said as she tried to piece the remaining uneaten portions of the harness together. She held up the remains of the harness that she had taped together.

"It looks pretty small," I said before she tried to place it on Miles. It didn't come close to clipping together around Miles chest, as there were as least six inches of orange vinyl harness missing.

"Try it again," I told Sarah, knowing all too well the clips wouldn't fasten together.

I remember that sinking feeling I felt in my stomach as I realized the potential problems in Miles' near future. The thought of him suffering from an intestinal foreign body made the pit in my stomach deeper.

Fortunately, the only good news was that he wasn't showing any ill effects of his ingestion. It's all good. He's fine. He's happy. He's normal. I tried all afternoon to give myself reassurance.

As a nervous Nellie, I couldn't rest, and by the early evening hours, I was pretty certain that Miles was feeling better than me. Having said that, I told Sarah it would be a good idea to bring him up the road to the emergency hospital for a quick evaluation that night. I figured it couldn't hurt to have a vet check him over, especially since he had just had a rough couple of days battling his kennel cough. Plus, I thought it would be good for my sanity since I was by myself, nearly 200 miles away, and feeling helpless in that situation.

My phone rang around 7 o'clock in the evening. That time it was an expected call from Sarah to let me know that she arrived at the emergency clinic. I reminded her to have the vet listen to Miles' lungs just to make sure that his kennel cough wasn't progressing. I wanted to make the most of the visit.

For the next twenty minutes, I paced around the apartment and waiting for a text message or a phone call to let me know what was going on. I thought the longer the visit, the greater the chance there was a problem. Finally, about forty-five minutes after my last call, my phone rang.

"You're never going to believe what happened," Sarah started. I turned my head to the side as I curiously leaned into the phone to hear the next sentence. *Here we go again.*

Knowing how restless I was, Sarah calmed my anxiety by first telling me of the doctor's findings.

"First off, the vet said that he's fine. Lungs sounded good. We're going to just monitor his poop at home to check for the harness, but if he vomits, we'll have to bring him back for an x-ray," Sarah explained.

I wasn't surprised by the vet's findings because Miles wasn't showing clinical signs. I knew that I would be able to sleep a little better. But I was curious what Sarah was going to say about what happened.

"It was a disaster getting him inside," Sarah told me. Now for anyone that has a dog or cat, more often than not, your pet does not enjoy visiting the vet. They just don't. They get nervous. They pee on the floor. They cower in the corner. In my world we call it the 'white-coat syndrome.' In other words, when they see the building from the outside or step foot under the sterile white lights, they change into a different animal. Some decide that they're just not going to walk one step further. Others become submissive. A few become aggressive. And then there was Miles.

After having witnessed Miles be given a few vaccines and have his nails clipped in the past, I should have known that this voyage wasn't going to be smooth and easy. How come everything with Miles was never straight forward, I wondered aloud. I stopped myself there. New place. New people. Oh, and that new place just so happens to be the vet hospital.

"Phil, he was out of control," Sarah started from the beginning. I sat down on the sofa as Sarah detailed her evening at the vet hospital.

Sarah had given the facility a call earlier to give them a heads up that our dog had munched on his harness and that she would be heading their way. When she arrived, Sarah left Miles in the car because she wanted to inform the front desk that Miles also had kennel cough. Rather than having him hack all over in their waiting room, she wanted to keep him isolated in the car until an exam room was available. Well, when Sarah mentioned to the secretary that Miles also had kennel cough, the woman stared at her from behind the front desk with an appalled, disgusted look. Umm, ma'am, it's a hospital, I would have said to her.

Sarah was literally the only person in the waiting room, and fortunately there was an exam room available right away. Of course, when she brought Miles inside from the car, he couldn't hold himself together. Another new place and as usual, he was out of his mind and had trouble listening to one word commands as he jumped on Sarah repeatedly. His excitement was reaching new levels and his pant picked up its pace within the once silent lobby. Sarah could only cringe as she helplessly awaited the unveiling of Miles hacking cough. *Please don't cough, please don't cough,* Sarah thought to herself as Miles lunged forward, pulling his collar tighter around his neck. He was in full pursuit of the receptionist as the door marked with a number one opened, revealing a new room for him to explore.

As the door shut behind her, Sarah leaned on the metal table to fill out some paperwork before the exam began. There was only one problem. She realized that she needed to bring the completed paperwork back out to the front desk. She looked down at Miles, who was already staring up at her with his open mouth and tongue to the side. If I had to guess, I'm pretty certain that he knew she would have to leave the room. As she opened the door and squeezed through the cracks, Miles made an unsuccessful attempt to escape as Sarah quickly sealed off the exit behind her. Well, as the old saying goes, if at first you don't succeed, try, try again. And with that in mind, Miles did just that as he plowed through the cracked opening of the door when Sarah tried to re-enter.

If Sarah thought it was embarrassing the first time Miles stepped foot into the lobby, then it just got a whole lot worse the second time. She chased after Miles into the lobby where he dodged between the chairs and weaved around the prescription food stand.

"Get over here," Sarah forcefully pronounced after she stepped on Miles' leash that he was dragging around the tile floor.

But within a second, Miles pulled back, twisted his neck, and alligator rolled his way out of the collar. Listening on the other end of the line, I didn't want to say anything, but I had always told her that his collar was too loose. However, at that moment, that was a moot point as I wouldn't dare say a word as Sarah continued to vent on her evening.

At that point Miles was completely naked, unrestrained, and running wild and free around... the entire hospital. He had moved on from the lobby and advanced his way to the pharmacy and the other hidden rooms behind the desk. The excitement was too much, and he started to cough, spewing viruses around the commonly walked hallways.

"I think he was running around the back room where they kept all of the bottled medicines," Sarah mentioned. I felt embarrassed for her.

She recalled chasing after Miles towards the front desk when she locked eyes with the menacing stare of the receptionist, who peered at her from just above the top of the countertop.

"Ma'am, you're going to need to put a leash on your dog," she impassively muttered in her mundane, gruff voice.

"Treat! Treat!" Sarah implored Miles as she tried to catch his attention with that key vocabulary word while acknowledging the request from Captain Obvious from behind the counter.

Within seconds of hearing that magic word, Miles was by Sarah's side and back in the exam room. I'm sure the only one that wanted Miles out of the hospital more than Sarah was indeed the hospital staff.

There was a knock on the door shortly after and a technician came in to assess Miles vitals. Do you honestly think Miles was going to let a random person take his temperature? That made two of us as I learned how Miles alligator-rolled yet again on the ground in an attempt to avoid any part of this exam. Sarah didn't think the technician obtained the heart rate or respiratory rate when she stepped out to report to the doctor. Hell with that, I'm sure she thought.

The best part of the night came when the vet told Sarah that Miles seemed fine, but that she would need to keep an eye on him at home for any problems. That was the end of the exam and undoubtedly enough for one day.

May 4, 2016.

Yes, you guessed it, my phone buzzed, alerting me that I just received a new text message. Bleary-eyed and tired, I scooted over to the edge of the bed and fumbled blindly on the end table for my phone. I could see the green light blinking, so I knew I had a new text message and wasn't just dreaming, though I wish I was. I slid my finger across the desktop screen.

4:40 AM.

Yes, that's right. It read 4:40 AM. Now let me ask you this. Who sends messages at that time at night, or should I say, morning. If I was in my twenties, maybe a college friend who was drunk-texting with one hand as he took a swig from the bottle with the other. Or perhaps a family member traveling overseas in Europe in a different time zone. But I think it's fair to say that it's pretty rare to be typing away on your phone at that time of day. Nothing positive comes at that hour.

So when I saw that Sarah texted me at that time, I knew all too well that it just wasn't going to be a good thing. I could only hope that message was going to read, "Hey! The Yankees won" or "What do you want to do tomorrow?" That eerie feeling crept into my insides as I read the message verbatim:

"Miles just threw up large chunk collar" followed by a wide-eyed emoji and an attached picture of the vomited, chewed-up six-inch piece of orange harness.

While I was relieved, I was actually more astonished that Miles held that weaved piece of vinyl in his stomach for over four days before he vomited it up. As usual he defied all odds and baffled my mind.

But in this case, it was more than welcomed. I felt the monkey on my back loosen its grip. Six days of anxiety had come and gone. My nerves felt at ease for the first time all week as my worry about Miles Murphy subsided, at least for the moment. And with my temporary piece of mind, I turned my phone to silent and fell back asleep.

CHAPTER 20

The Alpine Zone

"The long distance hiker, a breed set apart,
From the likes of the usual pack.
He'll shoulder his gear, be hittin' the trail;
Long gone, long 'fore he'll be back."
— M.J. Eberhart, author, photographer, and hiker

The topography of the White Mountains held true to form, as my hamstrings felt the slight burn from the nearly three mile hike along the Jewell Trail en route to the summit of Mount Washington, the highest peak in the Northeastern United States. The trees had noticeably thinned out and decreased in height as our terrain transitioned from the shaded, rocky, and heavily-wooded landscape that we had grown accustomed to over the past two-plus hours. The sugar maple, American beech and yellow birch that filled the northern hardwood deciduous forest had been filtered out by the evergreen conifers of the spruce-fir forest.

At an elevation of 3,000 feet, the temperatures had grown noticeably cooler so I decided that it was time to put on my long sleeve shirt. After taking a breather, I threw my backpack over my shoulder, and we continued the trek up the mountain. Beads of perspiration covered my brow as our journey became increasingly arduous, the blisters on my bunions torn open with each simultaneous lunge forward and step up. The pathway itself had grown noticeably wetter, narrower, and steeper as the once common red spruce became virtually non-existent to the eye, eventually being replaced by a forest of balsam firs, which signified that we were around 4,000 feet. With every stride the wind increased in intensity as a once faint breeze had now turned into a common gust. The increase in elevation was accompanied by the steady decline in height of the balsam firs. In fact, the forests had become noticeably stunted, forming a thicket on the perimeter that local hikers referred to as the 'tuckamore.' Trekking up the mountain, I was amazed that I could now see the tops of the trees, as the continual change in landscape provided a stark contrast to what we had seen at the base of the mountain earlier in the morning.

Though the trail and weather conditions changed as we progressed up the mountain, the one constant was Miles. That's right, he wasn't going to miss out on this voyage after he proved to us in previous days that both his endurance and aptitude were not up for debate as his willpower and mindset easily surpassed our greatest expectations. Pulling forward on the leash and itching to race forward, Miles never wavered as he led us along the trail for the entire morning. Navigating the slippery dirt terrain, steep topography and forest landscape, he never once sagged behind but acted as our guide by outlining to us the easiest path to traverse. Approaching 5,000 feet and noting that Miles was still going strong, I tugged on the leash as we approached a white sign nailed to a stake held upright between a couple of large rocks.

"Welcome to the ALPINE ZONE," I read the faded blue words aloud to Sarah. A cool, moist wind blew into my face from the northwest as I breathed in deeply and mentally recapped how I got to this point nearly a mile high in elevation.

For years, Sarah had told me that one of the things on her bucket list was to hike up Mount Washington. As an outdoors kind of person who loves nature, this was understandably right up Sarah's alley. So it was all but inevitable that when we moved up to Connecticut, we were going to head a few hours north to the Live Free or Die state. In the summer of 2016, we did just that and packed our bags for a long weekend vacation. In short, we hiked along numerous trails in New Hampshire including the cascades at the Arethusa Falls, all in preparation for our final day hike up Mount Washington.

We started that Monday morning off with a protein-packed breakfast at The Shack, a small log-cabin turned restaurant. While we ate our western omelets, we laughed as Miles unwaveringly stared at us from the car window. Poor guy. Even on vacation, his anxiety wouldn't allow him to take a day off.

When we drove the long road leading to the base of the mountain, Miles was going crazy in the backseat. His excitement was contained only by the roof and doors of the Subaru when we mercifully came to a halt in the parking lot. Driving with him bouncing around in the backseat is more than just distracting as you see his head bobbing up and down, left and right in the rear view mirror. Miles knew that we were in for another day of hiking based on our morning routine the past few days. He just didn't know the adventure he was about to take on.

Look, I'll be the first to admit that hiking is not my favorite activity. It's not that I don't like walking through the woods or exploring nature, but I find it to be tediously boring unless it is challenging. To give you another example, I'll bring up rafting. Floating down a river with category one rapids is ho-hum, but if you substitute those with category three or four, now we're talking. Looking up at the low clouds covering the upper third of its invisible peak, I knew that hiking up Mount Washington would be worth it when we looked down from the top at the incredible views below.

"We have to take the Jewell trail," Sarah shouted from ahead, signaling Miles and me to the area of woods across the Cog Railroad, where a coal-powered locomotive train from the 1860s was bringing people up the mountain. After seeing the train moving at what looked to be two miles per hour at a forty degree angle up the mountainside, I was more than happy to be walking on my own two feet up thousands of feet instead of relying on that aged cog railway.

Heading out past the train, our first challenge of the morning was learning that the Jewell trail started...across a river.

Sarah had told me that there was going to be a bridge. I didn't see a bridge. And neither did she. We didn't even know if this was a trail, let alone, 'the trail.'

Here we were, two minutes into our escapade going back and forth as to how Miles was going to cross the moving water.

"Let's just walk him across," Sarah suggested.

Staring at the slick rocks covered in water, some of which were completely submerged, I thought she was joking, or at least I hoped she was.

"Are you nuts, what if he breaks his leg or slips?" I responded. "Then what are we going to do? I'm just going to pick him up," I firmly stated.

"Good luck," Sarah muttered. "He's not going to let you. He's going to just alligator roll."

After bickering back and forth, I ended up walking along a tree that had fallen down across the river while Miles balanced himself on top of the rocks through the sixty degree water. That was the only time Miles followed for the rest of the day.

Our hike up the mountain started off smoothly as Miles quickly took the lead from the beginning, a position he didn't relinquish for the next five hours. The dirt trail up the mountainside, outlined with dense forest and green vegetation had some small rubble, exposed tree roots, and hairpin turns. We followed the white trail markers posted on the trees and continued along the designated path when all of a sudden I heard Sarah's voice from behind me.

"This doesn't look right." I glanced around and knew that something was out of place as the dirt trail had subtly been replaced by plants and foliage throughout. We continued navigating the makeshift trail while I peered ahead, scanning the area for those signature white trail markings all while hoping that the actual trail would soon reemerge from the wilderness.

I was ducking my head under the low tree branches and squirming my way around the innermost base of a birch tree trying to keep up with Miles who was five feet ahead. Fortunately the leash was only five feet otherwise he would have left us in the dust.

"We should probably head back," I said, noting the obvious as I turned around. But Miles stood still and focused. Facing the opposite direction, his eyes did not deviate from a fixed target.

I remember thinking how easily he would pull me down the mountain if it was a squirrel or other animal. I took one step in his direction, loosened the taut metal chain attached to his collar by just a few links, when he suddenly lunged.

"He has something!" Sarah remarked, racing over to help me pry open his mouth.

I had thought that he picked up a dead carcass. Sarah worried it was a black mushroom. Either way, whatever was in his mouth was not going to be good. I pried open his jaws and scraped out a mouthful of soft, brown muck.

Human feces.

To say that was disgusting would be an understatement as my hands and shirt sleeves were coated. There was a napkin crumbled up next to the pile of crap that Miles decided to uncharacteristically chow down on, which supported the fact that this wasn't from an animal, but from a person. And our dog had to discover it.

Now, waking up in the morning, did I expect Miles to uncover a pile of crap in the woods? No. And did I expect for us to have a smooth sailing, no problem kind of day with our dog? Of course not.

We backtracked our way from off the beaten path, yet the smell followed us, even after we washed our hands with our drinking water. That's hiking, I guess.

Reversing course about thirty feet, we weaved and dodged through the same patch of woods until we reached the main trail. From there, we saw where we had missed a turn, a quick switchback up the mountain to the left. The pathway upward from that point was no longer a smooth, steady incline like it was when we crossed the river earlier in the morning. The rocks covering the dusty trail were now softball sized and accompanied the gravel up this seemingly steeper pathway. That was the first time that I noticed the effects that elevation has on the mountainside terrain.

"Miles, do you want some water?" I asked aloud after spotting an area of cleared brush off of the main trail up ahead. I figured this makeshift camp site would be a good place to lay our bags down and take a breather. For a few minutes Sarah and I chit-chatted while taking a seat on a fallen tree trunk as Miles lapped up water from his collapsible dog bowl that we had packed. Soon enough though, his patience with us wore thin as he began to bark and prance back and forth, signaling to us that our break would need to give way to his uncontrollable energy. With a couple of Milk Bone treats I tried to entice our son to sit and be quiet, but I was nearly impaled by his front paws on my chest and knocked backwards off my perch at the site of his favorite cookies. It was clear that he was ready to keeping hiking at full throttle, so we packed up our water canteens and wisely let Miles take the lead.

As I described at the start of this chapter, it was as if each section of the mountain grew progressively steeper as we approached the Alpine Zone. And with each transition up the mountainside, I could not stop myself from talking to Sarah about Miles.

"It's absolutely amazing watching him," I spoke over my shoulder as we continued our ascension. "Every step, every movement is so precise," I noted for probably the third time that day. It was encouraging to see, as in the recent months of summer, the humidity really slowed Miles down on our walks, which made me start to wonder if it was all of the wear and tear on his joints paired with the effects of father time. He moved gracefully up the mountain, carefully placing each paw in the exact location it was intended while avoiding the sharp edges of rocks and maneuvering within the narrow margins whenever needed, all while keeping a keen eye for the whereabouts of his family. We were always trailing our leader, trying to place our two clumsy feet in the same spots that he had precisely placed his four. But I'd like to think that the reason we allowed Miles to take the lead was because I wanted to watch Miles artfully scale the mountain.

A sudden gust of wind whipped into my face, abruptly bringing me back to reality. My recollections of the morning were swiftly gone with the wind. The sign welcoming us to the Alpine Zone stared back as my thoughts shifted to the present task ahead.

Indeed, the terrain and landscape had progressively changed as we hiked the switchback trail over the course of three hours. From the time I read those faint blue letters on the white sign welcoming us to the Alpine Zone, it was like I suddenly changed mountains. Replaced by blue paint marks on boulders, the characteristic white tree trail markers were no longer existent, for there were no more trees due to the conditions brought on by the higher elevation. By now the path had significantly narrowed, boulders replaced rocks as moss and ferns replaced the tuckamore of balsam firs. But that didn't seem to bother Miles, whose energy only increased as he leaped up the sometimes two foot high stones that had slowly, yet steadily began to replace the dirt. Turning the corner, we came to a halt. I pulled back on his leash as I tried to balance myself on the moss-covered rock in the midst of a gusty crosswind.

Turning to see where Sarah was, I was easily distracted by the passing clouds to my left, the same clouds that I had seen covering the upper third of Mount Washington's peak from its base earlier in the morning. It was like a tale of two cities, as the windy, cool, misty terrain of the Alpine Zone above the clouds was a contrast to the heavily wooded, expansive land scanning the margins of my periphery from below. In the distance, I could make out the yellow Cog Railroad train descending the mountain. Looking at Miles, he was ready to go. His scorpion tail was raised and curled over his hind quarters. His front paws were placed in a skyward fashion on the rock ahead, his chest was thrust forward, and his eyes scanned the scenic views. With a simple 'let's go,' we were off once again.

But it wasn't going to be easy. Steps were turning into lunges as the cracks between the boulders were now wide gaps. I remember chuckling after thinking to myself, *do not fall, do not fall*, all while watching Miles walk like it was a leisurely Sunday morning stroll in the park.

Though I could see for miles, it was difficult to hear at distances greater than ten feet. I remembered checking out the terrain just a few paces ahead while Sarah stayed back with Miles. After a few lunges forward, I turned around and called back down to them. But my voice was carried away in the winds. I recalled the earlier weather report that stated winds would be approaching seventy miles per hour at the summit. Seeing how the conditions were changing and keeping in the back of my mind that we had our furry friend with us, I decided it was time to reverse course. We could have easily made it to the summit, but my concern was two-folded. What if Miles slipped and got hurt? And how would Sarah carry him down the mountain? Oh wait, that would be my job.

Miles didn't mind because he knew that he had the entire way down to hike. As long as he had somewhere to go, he was happy.

We carefully plodded our way down the moss surrounded rocks, crossed through the land of the balsam firs, traversed down the path between the evergreen conifers, and entered the dense, humid deciduous forest en route to the river. Even though it was the same trail, Miles was just as eager to be the leader and explore the land that he was heading down. Boundless energy. Awesome.

A part of me wanted to keep going because I was filled with relief that Miles still had the energy and stamina for such activities. Not that he was pushed to extremes on a daily basis, but to hike three days in a row for hours upon hours and not show any hint of fatigue was a welcomed sight.

We crossed the river, an expectedly delicate, cringe-worthy moment for me as I watched Miles shoulder deep in water stay poised and keep upright as he passed through the current. The conductor of the Cog Railroad, a woman in her early forties, was standing to the side of the locomotive, and I remember looking back as she commented how energetic Miles still was after seeing him earlier in the day.

"He's still ready to go!" she remarked. "How old is your puppy?" she asked.

"He's five," Sarah responded with a smile.

I had a grin on my face too, that is once I saw the open-mouthed impression that Sarah's response left on the face of the conductor. I'm not sure if she was surprised that he had this much energy at five years of age or the fact that it looked like he could hike the mountain a second time right then and there. Or perhaps, both.

We headed back to the parking lot and returned to our car. We had about a forty-five minute drive back to our cottage in the woods. Turning onto the highway, I turned around to see if Miles had curled up into his characteristic ball to take a well-deserved afternoon nap. A long day of hiking could do that to anyone, especially a dog that had to take twice as many steps as us humans.

Not this time. Instead he was standing, looking out the window, his pink tongue sagging to the side of his open mouth.

It was as if he was wondering, *where are we going to hike now?*

CHAPTER 21

BIOGRAPHY

"If you're doing a biography, you try to stay as accurate as possible to reality. But you really don't know what was going on in the person's mind. You just know what was going on in the minds of people around him."
— Clint Eastwood, film actor and director

We never really knew what to make of Miles' past. That is because we didn't have anything to go on. There was literally no history in his file when we picked him up from the shelter. All we knew was that he was from Kentucky. What happened in the previous two years of his life was up for speculation, but Sarah and I had put together our own theories and ideas over the past months and years as we composed his biography.

His story revolved primarily around his breed and his location. We think he lived out on a hundred-acre farm with more land than the eye could see. Knowing that Miles is part Border collie, we had always assumed that he enjoyed herding the cattle and sheep in the open pastures of the "Bluegrass State." And given the open land and the love of hunting shared by those in the Commonwealth, we could easily justify that his other half, Labrador retriever, was beyond serviceable as a hunting dog in the tall grasses filling the prairies. His white-tipped tail has always stood tall as Sarah and I ran alongside him at the beach or down the sidewalk, so why wouldn't it point to the sky as he darted through the meadows and grasslands under the watchful eye of his nearby hunters in the years past.

Now I mentioned above that we think he enjoyed herding sheep. Though we have brought him to farms in the past, we had never exposed him to such livestock. Having said that, I remember one day when he was sleeping on the couch when he heard the bleating cry of a sheep coming from the television in the background. He perked his ears at the initial 'baa,' but as the flock chimed in, the chorus of sounds from the herd caused Miles to abruptly jump off the sofa and run around the apartment barking. That's all I needed to see to tell myself that he had been around these domesticated farm animals somewhere along his journey in his early years. On a similar note, when Miles is around squirrels or rabbits, he goes crazy. Now if he comes across a deer in his path, whether it is on our walk or through the kitchen window of my mother-in-law's home, all bets are off. He gets even crazier, like to the point where you have to decide if the potential outcome of either whiplash or a separated shoulder is worth the risk of holding onto his leash.

Now this hasn't been the case with all farm animals that Miles has encountered. I think of the countless times that we traveled down to East Lyme to visit Sarah's mom. We would take him for a walk down the road and pass a couple of farms, but Miles never showed even the slightest interest in any of the horses we passed. It was a ho hum moment each and every time, which fed into our narrative that he lived amongst the horses on his Kentucky farm and the sight of these animals on an everyday basis turned into just another mundane encounter. And unlike the sheep that we assumed he had worked and herded, he had no working interaction with the horses, thus, the interest or excitement just wasn't there. Now let's say hypothetically his duties included herding wild mustangs across the grassland. I'd like to believe that the sight of those 1200-pound stallions would have caused him to become somewhat invigorated and enlivened upon passing them at those farms in East Lyme, but it never did.

For squirrels and rabbits, I think these are just different animals, or friends as Sarah likes to refer to them as, that he had never met or been around until moving to New Jersey. Besides Miles, who would possibly know, right? But it didn't take us long to learn that there wasn't a single one that Miles didn't want to chase.

Given his unknown history, it's somewhat enjoyable to try and put the pieces together from his past by looking how he lives in the present. Take for example his separation anxiety. Why is it that he can't be alone in the apartment for more than thirty seconds without barking, racing around, or tearing up shoes, purses, and essentially anything he can get his jaws on? But if you put him in the car, you could easily forget he was inside as he often curls up into a ball and takes a nap on the back seat without ever making a peep...for hours. Perhaps it fits into my wife's narrative that he was abandoned by the passing of his elderly owner inside their 'old Kentucky home' and now associates houses with sadness, isolation, and desertion. Perhaps that's why our Kentuckian loves taking a ride with us in our car, because he quickly learned that the few initial occurrences of motion sickness associated with this novel mode of transportation would eventually be replaced by the constant security of his family's love, the occasional 'on the road' Milk Bone snack and the reassurance that his folks would always come back to rescue him.

Even for dogs, and in our case Miles, figuring out one's past can be a challenging feat, but if successful it can help provide an understanding of yesteryear while providing a greater insight into tomorrow. And with that, I will simply say the following.

This has been the story, or I guess you could say, the biography of the early years for the best dog we've ever had, and as Sarah likes to remind me, the *only* dog we've ever had, Miles Murphy.

Remember That Time When...

"Take care of all your memories. For you cannot relive them."
- Bob Dylan, American singer-songwriter

"How are you going to finish the book," Sarah asks as she pours herself a cup of coffee.

It is a Saturday morning in early September 2016 when Sarah raises that question. She has been intrigued ever since I started reading her the chapters in recent weeks. And it got me thinking. How am I going to write the final chapter?

Sitting in the family room of our new Connecticut apartment, I take a moment and think about how we got to this point. I begin to rehash the past handful of years and how our dog played a big part in our daily lives. It had never been my intention to write a book about Miles. In fact, it never even crossed my mind, that is until I saw the impact that Miles had on my family and friends. And with that, I decided the book would not only detail the everyday ups and downs of having a dog, but the unique impact that those times had on our lives. I simply wanted to tell a story about life and how our dog influenced ours.

Gazing out through the sliding door window I see a black Labrador puppy panting and pulling his owner down the sidewalk. I couldn't help but smile as I signal for Sarah to take a look at the all too familiar scene.

There was a lot going through my mind on that Indian summer morning as I pulled out my laptop to begin writing the final chapter of this book. There have been a handful of instances over the years where Miles made us scratch our heads, become red in the face, jump off the couch, or even give him an occasional, but well-deserved 'timeout.' But there have been so many more everyday joys that have made us laugh and smile on a daily basis. I couldn't write a chapter about each example, but here are a few that I hope you enjoy.

Remember that time when...

...I was in the shower, peering through the steam covered glass door at the silhouette of Miles on the carpet outside of the bathroom. I thought he was grooming his paws, but without having my glasses on, I couldn't make out a clear picture. I wish I had my frames on because it turned out that he was chewing my flip phone into, I don't know, twenty-three pieces. Yes, I counted them because I tried to put the puzzle together to ensure that he didn't have any metal or plastic inside of his stomach. Plus, the battery was punctured, so why not just add the concern of oral burns from the leaking battery acid to this veterinarian's anxiety list. It turned out that he was okay. I guess that was just his way of saying, "Hey Dad, it's time to get a smart phone. It's 2015."

How about the time when Miles surprised us all and behaved well on Christmas Eve at my mother-in-law's home. Come on, by now you should know that he has never been able to contain himself on any holiday. Between the food and all the people, there were just way too many temptations. And on that night before Christmas in 2015, Miles pushed the limits in more than one way. While family was talking in the kitchen, Miles jumped up onto the counter and grabbed an entire twelve ounce New York Strip Steak without anyone noticing in that moment. We only knew after Sarah's brother rhetorically asked, "I thought there were three steaks?" as we all stared at a plate of two while Miles stared upwards and licked his lips.

Miles was always good at discreetly surveying the area prior to striking at that well-calculated, opportunistic moment. And sometimes that left me with an uncomfortable feeling, including on that Christmas Eve night on which I soon found myself driving down the road to the local pharmacy, picking up a bottle of hydrogen peroxide, and giving Miles a couple of tablespoons of this emetic with a turkey baster. Sarah helped hold Miles outside on the front lawn while the entire family watched from the kitchen windows. So much for a relaxing holiday. The fear that he would vomit, have explosive diarrhea, and potentially develop pancreatitis from ingesting this fat-filled piece of meat entered my mind, but incredibly, it never happened. If there was going to be a dog that escaped that diagnosis, I'm happy Miles was the one. Of course, his appetite didn't stop there as he once again gave in to those luring forces later in the night when he jumped on top of the reclaimed pine dining room table to eat some turkey left on a plate. There he was, standing on the red tablecloth in the middle of the room, and all I could do was stare at him from the other side of the house. It was like a slow-motion event that happened in the blink of an eye. And the only thing that amazed me more than him not getting sick was that Mrs. Aupperlee invited him to come back to her home for Christmas Eve dinner next year.

Speaking of Christmas Eve, what about the year before when my dad called me on Christmas Day to complain about all the fur that Miles had left behind when I put him in the backseat of his Sonata in the garage the night before. If you recall, Miles was barking nonstop at dinner so I had to put him in timeout. Well, if my dad was upset by the fur, he was infuriated when he learned that Miles had gnawed on and severed his driver-side seat belt, leaving behind the vinyl remnants and a $400 repair bill. Dear Grandpa, Merry Christmas. Love Miles.

I remember when Miles would plunge his head into the laundry basket and race around the apartment with a sock or a t-shirt in his mouth as he looked for attention. It became part of his daily routine for weeks at a time. Whether in the morning when Sarah or I were watching the news or at night when we were making dinner, if Miles was restless or wanted to go outside, running around with a pair of underwear would be his way of grabbing our attention, getting us off the couch or out of the kitchen.

What about the first time we witnessed devil dog mode? Or how about when Sarah's eighty-five-year-old grandparents had that same experience...in their home! Yeah, that was pretty cringe-worthy. Or the occasions when he picked up a live chipmunk and a dead squirrel in his mouth, before I proceeded to drive him down the road for a rabies vaccine booster? And I can't forget the times when Sarah took Miles out for a walk, and all I would hear was 'stop, stop' coming from the apartment hallway as the sounds of nails scraping the walls and rattling chains emanated from behind our front door. Only with Miles.

The list could go on and on as we rehash all the stressful moments that our dog has given us over the years. From the havoc he wreaked on a weekly basis to the everyday life changes he forced us to make to confront his separation anxiety, Miles has never fallen short in making each and every day interesting.

But let me ask you this: whoever said the best dog needed to be a perfect dog?

For us, nothing could ever come remotely close to replacing Miles and the special joy he has provided us each and every day. The memories are impossible to forget and a pleasure to recall.

I remember on day one when Sarah established the rule, "No dogs in the bed or on the couch."

And I remember on night one when Miles planted his flag on the sofa and mattress. He clearly didn't get Sarah's memo. Nor was it enforced. I guess rules are meant to be broken.

I remember when I would come home from work in our first apartment in New Jersey. Sarah would be working the overnight shift, so it was just me and Miles many a night. Regardless of the time that I came home or the stress brought on throughout the day, his priceless evening routine would always bring a smile to my face. He would prance around his wire-framed crate, which rocked back and forth with each excited step, as he waited for me to open the gates to freedom. And every time that cage-front door opened, he would race down the hallway with his head held high and drool-covered Kong clenched in the back of his mouth as he characteristically panted and shook his body from head to tail with excitement that his dad was finally home.

I remember when my mom was in the hospital and the smiles he brought to her face every time she looked at his bedside picture. And the delight he gave to my dad, which provided my father with a much-anticipated break from reality at each visit. Speaking of my parents, I remember how Miles would excitedly burst through the front door at the welcomed sight of 'grandpa' but would instantly become gentle and reserved as he carefully greeted 'grandma.' It's like he always knew who he was around, or in other words, when he could be his crazy self.

I remember how Miles would share the couch with me on football Sundays and watch every Giants game.

But not until he joined Sarah and me earlier in the morning for our much anticipated and timely seasonal apple picking, pumpkin picking, and Christmas tree hunting experiences...

I remember when he joined us on vacation and overcame his fear of waves at Cape May.

And I remember when he helped me battle my fear of heights when we hiked up Mount Washington.

I remember every May when Miles devoured the home-made carrot-apple-peanut butter 'pupcakes' that we made to celebrate each of his birthdays with us.

Speaking of food, how could I forget the pools of drool and mouthwatering attentiveness brought on by the sounds of his crunchy Chicken and Rice kibble filling his stainless steel bowl. But it isn't just the slick kitchen floors or Miles' keen focus at breakfast or dinner that makes me smile, but his customary post-meal, tail-wagging appreciation as he races over to say 'thank you' for yet another splendid feast.

I remember when we gave him his different nicknames over the years. From Little Buddy to Murphs to even MurphMan, we have a story that explains why he has earned each of his titles and a weekly reminder as to why he hasn't lost any of them either.

I remember the times he cheered us up.

I remember when we needed it most, Miles was there to comfort us and bring a reassuring smile to our faces.

I remember the times when his wild behavior caused us to laugh because becoming angry would do us no good.

I remember this experience, that event and when this happened and that took place.

I remember all there is to remember that deserves to not be forgotten.

Unfortunately, I cannot forget how quickly these early years have soared on by. I'll be the first to acknowledge that sharing these memories brings a smile to my face, but also a solemn realization that as the months tick along, father time continues to watch from above. Of course, we cannot relive the past memories, but we can rejoice with the thoughts that there will be plenty more mind-boggling, head-scratching moments to laugh about and heartwarming times to share with our family, friends, and of course, Miles Murphy.

But these future anticipations and expectations are a direct result of the past recollections and daily experiences, for I am reminded every day how great this unique dog has been to us. Miles' loyalty, faithfulness, and genuineness have made him more than just another four-legged domesticated canine, but an irreplaceable member of our family with an unbreakable bond.

It's been quite the journey...

As I sit back in my chair, I glance up at the clock above the end table where Miles' leash lays patiently. 11:00 AM. Wow, time flies.

With that in mind, I realize fairly quickly that it's now time to take Miles outside for his long overdue morning walk. Without making eye contact, I can feel his unwavering stare, hear the sound of his grumble, and indirectly make out his white tipped tail thrashing back and forth across the carpet from the corner of my eye. I close my laptop.

"WOOF!" A characteristic solitary bark erupts.

Some things just never change, I think to myself, as a smile crosses my face.

And that's okay with me.

Miles laying down in the sun-filled backseat of Sarah's Subaru. It's his favorite spot to relax, that is if you exclude our sofa and our bed, or should I say, *his sofa* and *his bed*.

Talk about a vocal backseat driver. If Miles wasn't closing his eyes for a nap or smelling the outside air through an open window, he would be co-piloting from his central position in the backseat.

Visiting my parents always puts a smile on our faces. And yes, that's Miles sitting on his Grandpa's green, well-manicured front lawn...

On our vacation in Cape May, Miles would love to run back and forth on the beach, but would always make time for a photo.

Even Miles enjoyed the sunset at the tip of Cape May's peninsula as we strolled along the beach at day's end.

A hot summer jog in the park...

...followed by a game of fetch.

Advice: Do not hold onto the frisbee for too long.

(Above and below) – Autumn is Miles' favorite season. Cool temperatures and low humidity equates to long walks on the trails and in the mountains.

Miles' couch. Need I say more.

Looking out of the window for his folks to come home is part of Miles' everyday routine.

Guilty, very guilty.

Celebrating Miles' May birthday with an annual batch
of apple-peanut butter 'pupcakes' helped bring
about his best behavior (above and below).

November 6, 2015 – Our wedding picture is one our favorites
because it included Miles on the best day of our lives.
(Photo Courtesy of Matt Branscombe, BSC Photo)

November 6, 2015 – Scott helped manage my emotions
along with Miles as we walked down the processional
on our wedding day. Hold on tight Scott... (Photo
Courtesy of Matt Branscombe, BSC Photo)

November 6, 2015 – Miles was well-behaved and stayed preoccupied with his peanut butter stuffed bone on our wedding day. (Photo Courtesy of Matt Branscombe, BSC Photo)

On a hike in New Hampshire, Miles poses with
Sarah for a quick photo near the waterfall.

Happy to be on a hike, Miles' would only like to take
a short break before continuing along the path.

Mount Washington – the Alpine Zone. Miles
never missed a step as our tour guide.

There were thousands of Christmas trees at this farm, and we saw each and every one of them on yet another early winter Sunday.

Even Santa knows it's best to move over during devil-dog mode. Soon after, as if he were at home, Miles made himself quite comfortable on the couch at his great-grandparents' house.

Walking in a winter wonderland with my sled dog...

"Good Dog." Our first picture of Miles
always puts a smile on our faces.

Printed in the United States
By Bookmasters